P9-DWG-205

QUIVER TREES,
PHANTOM ORCHIDS
& ROCK SPLITTERS
THE REMARKABLE SURVIVAL
STRATEGIES OF PLANTS

JESSE VERNON TRAIL

ecw Press

Copyright © Jesse Vernon Trail, 2015

Published by ECW Press
665 Gerrard Street East
Toronto, Ontario M4M 1Y2
416-694-3348 • info@ecwpress.com

Cover design: Tania Craan
Cover images: Ponderosa Pine © Alloy Photography/Veer
Author photo: Cheryl M. Trail
Back cover images: Jesse Vernon Trail

LIBRARY AND ARCHIVES CANADA
CATALOGUING IN PUBLICATION

Trail, Jesse Vernon, author
Quiver trees, phantom orchids & rock splitters: the remarkable survival strategies of plants / Jesse Vernon Trail.

Issued in print and electronic formats.
ISBN 978-1-77041-208-8 (pbk)
ISBN 978-1-77090-703-4 (pdf)
ISBN 978-1-77090-704-1 (epub)

1. Plants—Hardiness. 2. Plants—Effect of stress on. 3. Plant ecology.

I. Title. II. Title: Quiver trees, phantom orchids and rock splitters.

QK754.T73 2015   581.7
C2014-907627-4   C2014-907628-2

The publication of *Quiver Trees, Phantom Orchids and Rock Splitters* has been generously supported by the Government of Canada through the Canada Book Fund and by the Government of Ontario through the Ontario Book Publishing Tax Credit and the Ontario Media Development Corporation.

PRINTED AND BOUND IN CANADA   Printing: Friesens 5 4 3 2 1

This book is dedicated to Cheryl,
my partner in life, for her steadfast
support and friendship,
and to my wonderful son, Matt.

AUTHOR'S NOTE

Before we set out to discover plants, their habitats and adaptations around the world, we begin with a brief introduction to the naming of plants — taxonomy. Simply put, taxonomy is a way to organize or classify the many different plants that exist. Taxonomy is a science unto itself, and a book-length subject, but we will do our best to keep things as brief and clear as possible.

In the grocery store, fruits and vegetables are placed into different groups. There are salad vegetables like tomatoes, cucumbers and lettuce; root vegetables like carrots, potatoes and parsnips; and in another section, the fruits — apples, oranges, berries and so on. You'll note that citrus fruits are further categorized by their kinds, such as oranges, grapefruits and lemons. Apples are in the same area, with the different varieties — such as Golden Delicious, Granny Smith and Spartan — kept in separate bins. This is simple organizing, which is what the naming of plants is essentially all about.

In botany there are eight main taxonomic groups (or ranks), as follows:

1. *Domain*: all organisms
2. *Kingdom*: either plant or animal
3. *Division or Phylum*: angiosperms (flowering plants) and gymnosperms (plants that produce naked seeds)
4. *Class*: groups of closely related orders (class 1 is monocots; class 2 is dicots)
5. *Order*: groups of closely related families
6. *Family*: a grouping of related genera; may consist of a few to many genera (example: the rose family or the grass family)
7. *Genus*: a group consisting of one or more similar species
8. *Species*: a group of closely related, mutually fertile individuals; the basic unit of plant classification

We are mainly concerned with family, genus and species, along with a few lower rankings or groups. Genus and species are frequently further classified by vegetative traits viii or characteristics.

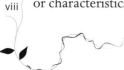

Take *Bellis perennis* as an example: *Bellis* is the genus (or genera), and *perennis* is the species. This genus and the species identified belong to the *Asteraceae Compositae* family.

Cultivars, varieties (*var.*), subspecies (*subsp.* or *ssp.*) and hybrids offer further differentiation, but they're of secondary importance for our purposes. Subspecies may have developed because of geographical or environmental differences that formed and were observed in plants of a species. Varieties have unique features that are different from the species, usually related to appearance. Hybrids are between two species in the same genus, or infrequently between two different genera.

Now, with this in mind, let's get to what these plants can do.

CHAPTER ONE

POLLINATION AND ATTRACTING POLLINATORS

Flowers, despite their beauty, are above all utilitarian: their primary purpose is to produce seeds. Some basic botany in a nutshell: the plant produces flowers; the flowers are pollinated by a pollinator; the flower is fertilized; the flower then produces seed; the seed is spread; the seed germinates and develops into a new plant; and voilà, the species lives on.

The sex life of plants resembles that of most of the earth's creatures, as the male pollen is transferred to the female receptive or reproductive organs, including the flower's ovary. It's a cycle that repeats over and over, with new flowers emerging from the new plants. And there is a reward for the pollinator, who is gifted with food nectar and protein-rich pollen, which benefits bees and some other creatures as well.

Our focus here is on the flowering plants, angiosperms, though similar processes occur among other plants as well. Flowering plants have developed some fascinating survival strategies to ensure that their flowers are attractive to potential pollinators. Many plants produce sweet nectar in their flowers to attract creatures, while other plants use fragrance as a lure. Still others rely on color or wonderful shapes to attract their visitors — or any combination of these strategies.

In some instances, the flowering plant and the pollinator become partially or fully dependent on each other. In other instances, wind, water and other means achieve the pollination requirements. In the cases of plants such as holly, each plant is either male or female. For such dioecious plants, both sexes have to be in the vicinity of the other. If not, pollination, fertilization and seed production cannot take place. Other plants, meanwhile — monoecious varieties — have both male and female flowers. The majority of flowering plants, however, have both sexes (stamen and pistil) within each flower, but pollination must be transferred from one flower to the next for fertilization to occur.

Of course, we humans also benefit from these fascinating processes. Think of the exquisite aroma of a rose, a spectacular vista of vividly colored flowers carpeting the landscape or the intricate shapes and colors of a passion vine. We even enjoy the activities of the pollinators and the entire flowering process.

Let's begin by focusing on the remarkable process of pollination and explore some of the main pollinators and their often special relationships with flowers.

INTRODUCING *the* POLLINATORS

BEES *and* WASPS

Bees are immensely important in the pollination of a great many flowering plants. They are virtually indispensable when it comes to the majority of our food crops, not to mention animal life. Thus it is a matter of great concern that many bee species are under threat and face possible extinction. This would be a severe blow not only to mankind, but also to a tremendous number of animals, insects and plant species as well.

All bees are partial to flowers in the blue, purple and ultraviolet shades that dominate one end of the color spectrum, but bumblebees find blue flowers especially attractive. Scientists have determined that bees see a broader portion of the color spectrum than we do. They may well see a pure white flower as having a vivid, highly attractive color we cannot see, which is perhaps why they are also strongly drawn to white flowers.

3

The relationship between certain species of orchid — especially *Ophrys* — and bees is special. Each flower has the almost uncanny appearance of the shapely body (from a bee's perspective) of a female bee. Male bees are duped by the perceived potential for sex. As if this is not enough, these orchids also exude a perfumelike scent that simulates the pheromones produced by receptive female bees. The male bees are either very slow learners or enjoy the experience, since they continue on to the next flower.

Many of these mimicking orchids target specific bees, wasps or other insects to ensure pollination of their flowers. For example, carefully observe the British bee orchid, *O. mellifera*, and the yellow bee orchid, *O. lutea*, and you will see the close similarity to the female bee or other insect being mimicked. However, there is a danger to the plant in targeting specific insects: without the presence of this particular insect, pollination of the orchid would not take place and the very existence of the species would be in great peril.

The grasslands of central England provide one habitat for the bee orchid, *Ophrys apifera*. Notice the flower's intricate design looks very similar to a female bee. When the male bee lands, he grasps on to the thick velvety maroon-and-yellow lower lip of the flower in an attempt to copulate with it. In the process, the upper flower above the bee dusts the bee's head with pollen. The bee then carries this pollen

4

to the next flower, where the pollen is received, and pollination is successful.

Ophrys apifera, bee orchid DR. AMADEJ TRNKOCZY

Instead of using mimicry, other plants, such as *Catalpa speciosa*, have intricate designs on their flowers that act like a flight-landing platform to guide a bee or other insects to their nectar and pollen. Each of this tree's flowers has a broad lower-lip landing pad, inviting the insect to its nectar with markings of orange lines and rows of purple dots.

Many of us are unaware of the great distances that bees travel in a single day to collect nectar and pollen from flowers. Some will even travel high into the Himalayan mountains to dine on the nectar of densely woolly *Saussurea gossypiphora* and *S. sacra*. Weary after a hard day's work, bees often find refuge from the extremely cold mountain nights in these particularly accommodating plants. Several species of *Saussurea* are so furry that bees can cozy up deep inside, where the flowers

5

Icy *Saussurea gossypiphora*, shot in the Himalaya PRATEEK/CC-BY-SA-2.5

are, and stay overnight in the warmth of their shelter. The plants even provide a small opening at the top, allowing the bees to enter and reach the flowers — it's deluxe hotel accommodation for the bees.

By covering themselves with downy hairs, several *Saussurea* species are better able to endure the harsh conditions found in the Himalaya. Often, the plants are so densely

6

woolly that it is difficult to distinguish the leaves within the mound of fur that provides the ultimate in insulation.

HUMMINGBIRDS *and* OTHER BIRDS

Of all the birds that pollinate flowers, hummingbirds are among the most amazing. For such tiny birds they move incredibly fast, and when they hover to sip sweet nectar from a flower, their rapid wing beats are but a blur. Many species of hummingbird are also quite colorful, which only adds to their appeal. By flitting about from flower to flower, they are very efficient pollinators of several different flowering plants, and in return hummingbirds find a good source of sweet food nectar.

Hummingbirds are some of the best pollinators for flowers with long floral tubes, such as the flowers of the trumpet vine. Nectar is often accessible only by birds or insects with long proboscises like those of our hummingbirds. Reds and oranges are especially attractive to hummingbirds, as these birds see more toward the red end of the color spectrum. Hummingbirds have a poor sense of smell, so flower fragrance is not a factor in attracting them.

High on the slopes of the Andes Mountains in Colombia, we can feel the coolness of the moist air, as well as see the thick fog all around us. Among the dense green foliage of the forest lives an extremely rare, nearly extinct, exquisitely

7

beautiful species of passionflower vines, *Passiflora parritae*. Climbing by tendrils high into the trees, this vine bears a profusion of large upside-down hanging clusters of bright orange flowers in August and September.

The sole pollinator of this magnificent passionflower is the tiny sword-billed hummingbird, *Ensifera ensifera*. It is also the only bird on earth with a bill longer than its body, excluding the tail. Mainly because of global warming, this hummingbird is being forced to even higher altitudes, leaving the passionflower without its pollinator. The hummingbird might still survive by sipping on the nectar of other flowering plants higher up the mountain slopes, but the passionflower is faced with possible extinction. Even propagation attempts to save *Passiflora parritae* have failed. There is, however, one known specimen in cultivation in the San Francisco Botanical Garden at Strybing Arboretum. If you are ever in the area, do pay it a visit.

In a starkly different climate, the hot fynbos of the South African Cape in summer is home to the magnificent and often colorful large flowers of *Protea* species and their main — in some circumstances exclusive — pollinator, the Cape sugarbird. The King protea, *Protea cynaroides*, is South Africa's floral emblem. It is a medium-sized woody shrub with leathery green leaves, but it is its flower that is most incredible for its intricate structure. Each of the

Passiflora parritae, passionflower vine JOANNE TAYLOR

many flower heads of these striking plants is huge. The dense, clustered central zone is white, cream or yellowish, surrounded by showy bracts (modified, often showy leaves accompanying flowers) that vary in color from deep crimson to shades of pink.

The protea flowers are perfect for the Cape sugarbirds, supplying them with plenty of sweet nectar in return for their pollination service. Sugarbirds are gray-brown with a spot of bright yellow under their tails, and the males have

9

impressively long tail feathers. A long sharp beak with a long rough-tipped tongue allows the birds to reach the rich nectar of the protea.

There are many more examples of hummingbird and other bird pollinators, but these two demonstrate the strong relationships that can exist between flowering plants and birds.

BUTTERFLIES *and* MOTHS

Like the bee and the hummingbird, the butterfly and the moth also have a proboscis to sip the sweet nectar of flowers. Butterflies, for the most part, are out and about during the daylight hours, whereas the moth, depending on its species and the species of plant being visited, may feed only at night. Like bats, evening- and night-feeding moths are most often attracted to flowers with a strong fragrance. The flowers of these plants are usually a pale color or white.

Just a small sampling of some of the better-known butterfly- and moth-pollinated flowering plants include butterfly bush, *Buddleia davidii*, and milkweed, *Asclepias*, visited often by specific butterfly species. Evening star, *Mentzelia decapetala*, and certain species of queen of the night, such as *Hylocereus* and *Selenicereus*, open their flowers only after sundown and often to attract a particular moth pollinator.

Certain species of succulents and cacti of arid regions

have exclusive symbiotic relationships with specific moths. For example, only yucca moths can pollinate yuccas, and yucca flowers are the sole source of food for the moth larvae. Amazingly, there is one species of moth for each species of yucca. The yucca moths lay their eggs in the yucca flowers and in the process collect pollen that they transfer to the next flower, and so on. The developing moth larvae feed on both the nectar and, as they get older, some of the maturing seeds as well. There is no danger of all the seeds being eaten, as hundreds of seeds are produced; many seeds remain for later dispersal to start new plants. Adult moths, in return for their pollination service, get food from the abundant nectar in the yucca flowers.

BATS

Bats are nocturnal creatures that feed mostly on insects, but they also supplement their diets with the sweet-tasting, nutritious nectar of certain evening- and night-blooming flowers. Bats cannot see very well, so the best way for a flowering plant to attract bats is with strong fragrance and/ or large, easily accessible flowers, rather than flower color.

Found in an arid region not far from the central coast of Mexico, the strongly fragrant century plant, *Agave americana*, is prized by bats and humans when in bloom. Virtually all agaves are monocarpic, meaning they die after a single

11

flowering, but when they do bloom, it is a spectacular display. From the familiar agave stemless rosette of spiny gray-green or bluish-green tapered leaves grows a huge flower stalk with symmetrical branching. Yellowish-green to bright yellow flowers cluster at the end of each branch. Wildlife feed on the century plant's copious nectar during the day, but one of the plant's main pollinators, the fruit bat, visits at night, darting quickly from one flower to the next, ensuring the transfer of pollen.

The tropical Monteverde cloud forest region of Costa Rica is home to the bat-pollinated *Mucuna* vine. It bears long rope-like stalks that hang below the forest canopy, where night-flying bats can easily access its deliciously fragrant blossoms. These pea-like flowers in large dense clusters are often brilliantly colored in reds, yellows, purples and more, depending on the species.

Other night-blooming, bat-pollinated flowering plants include the organ pipe cactus, *Stenocereus thurberi*, with its long, tubular musky-scented flowers; the Arizona saguaro cactus, *Carnegiea gigantea*; and various species of the queen of the night.

FLIES

We don't often think of pollinators beyond those essential Bs: birds, bees, butterflies and bats, but other insects have a

role to play as well. Flies, for example, are often attracted to flowers emanating the stench of rotting meat or other unpleasant smells. Two prominent examples, both from Southeast Asia, are the giant flowers of *Rafflesia arnoldii* and the titan arum, *Amorphophallus titanium*. The *Rafflesia* and related genera and species, such as *Stapelia* and *Hoodia*, take aroma to the most extreme level of repulsiveness. Several species also have the coloring and marbled patterns of fatty, rotting meat. Sounds and smells delicious — but only to a fly, that is! (Keep in mind, though, that many flies are also attracted to more pleasant scents.)

Rafflesia arnoldii has the largest single flower in the world. Each flower can measure up to 3 feet in diameter. Often referred to as carrion flowers, a common name shared by the other related genera and species, *Rafflesia arnoldii* are parasitic on nearby host plants and can be seen only when in bloom; otherwise the plants are hidden beneath the soil surface.

Another similar plant you might not want in your garden can be found in the forests of southern France. The *Aristolochia rotunda*'s solitary, long, upright, tubular flower is a greenish yellow, with a distinctive maroon to deep purple upper flap. Its stench lures the flies inside, and they crawl down the flower tube. The inside of the tube has long downwardly directed hairs that are dense at the base to prevent the flies from crawling out. After a day or

13

Aristolochia rotunda DR. AMADEJ TRNKOCZY

so confined inside the flower, the struggling flies become covered with pollen and are allowed to escape when the plant's tubular hairs loosen. Fortified by nectar, the insects fly off and pollinate the next flower they visit.

EXPLORING OTHER MEANS *of* POLLINATION

WIND *and* WATER

Hay fever and allergy sufferers are well aware of wind-pollinated plants and when and where their pollen is in the air. Wind-pollinated plants include beech, birch, elm, poplar, goldenrod, oak, hazelnut, nettle, walnut and pine. Grass family members are usually wind-pollinated as well. In each case, it is the male flowers that produce the often copious amounts of pollen to be transferred by air. But pollen transfer by bees and other creatures is a much more direct and efficient process than the random dispersal by wind.

14

In the Northern Okanagan Valley of British Columbia in spring, the ground can become carpeted by the bright yellow pollen of tall ponderosa pines, *Pinus ponderosa*. It is beautiful to see, and it also demonstrates the huge amount of pollen these pines need to produce to increase the chances that female flowers will receive the pollen.

Most aquatic plants are water-pollinated, producing a large amount of pollen to drift on the water currents. Again, much of the pollen is wasted.

SELF-POLLINATION

With a small number of flowering plant species, self-pollination can occur, thus circumventing the natural sex life of plants. But this is far from the norm in the plant world — and some would even say it's an unnatural occurrence. When it does happen, it is often a reaction to environmental circumstances or a lack of pollinators in the area over time.

15

CHAPTER TWO

SEEDS AND THEIR DISPERSAL

After pollination and fertilization, flowers produce seeds that are dispersed to enable the continuation (growth) of most flowering plant species.

Seed size and shape vary considerably, as does the quantity produced by each plant. The containers or capsules that contain a plant's seeds also come in an almost infinite variety of shapes and sizes, though fruits, nuts, pods and cones are the main types. Animals (including man), birds and other wildlife enjoy eating these and unwittingly disperse a plant's seeds, often to great distances.

Many plants use fascinating methods to disperse their seeds, including catapult-like ejection, hitchhiking, parachutes or even planting their own seeds. Other plants require just the right circumstances for even one of their many seeds to germinate. Some produce seeds with exceptionally hard coats or incredible viability. We'll explore these clever adaptations that help ensure future generations.

ASTRONOMICAL SEED QUANTITIES

The dry tropical forests of northern Venezuela are home to a special epiphytic orchid often referred to as the American swan orchid, *Cycnoches chlorochilon*. An epiphyte is a plant that is rooted not in the soil, but on the surfaces of other plants and trees. In late summer, the swan orchid is in full bloom, displaying large, fragrant greenish-yellow blossoms that are delightfully intricate in form.

Once fertilized, the blossom develops a seed capsule filled with some of the smallest seeds known. According to a report from the late 1940s, the count of microscopic seeds in a single capsule of our particular orchid species, *Cycnoches chlorochilon*, was found to be an incredible 3,770,000. This count was conducted at the Royal Greenwich Observatory in England — an appropriate location, considering the astronomical quantity of seeds! Even the seed capsules of the common florist's orchid, *Cymbidium* species, can contain up to 1.5 million seeds.

Unlike the seeds of most plants, the tiny orchid seeds contain virtually no reserves of food. To develop into plants, orchids depend on a complex set of favorable circumstances.

17

One such circumstance is that they must meet up with the right sort of fungus to promote germination and growth of seeds into young plants. They also require ideal soil, moisture, temperature and a sheltered location. With such precise requirements, it is a wonder that any seed germinates at all. But just imagine how prolific and widespread orchids would be if each and every one of their millions of seeds germinated and grew into full-size plants. Can you imagine orchids as exquisitely beautiful weeds, covering the landscape as far as the eye can see?

GRANITE-HARD SEED COATS
and OTHER SPECIAL REQUIREMENTS

Most plants supply their seeds with a storehouse of food before sending them out into the world. They also provide them with some often remarkable protective means to help ensure their survival. Seed embryos will not emerge from their protective casing until outside conditions are just right. Some require light and some dark before germination and growth can occur. Most need the presence of moisture. Some require up to several years of freezing and thawing, while others remain dormant only through the hot summer months, and still others require the presence of fire or intense heat before they open. A few plant species require abusive means such as scraping, chipping or even cutting of the seed capsule. Some need to be soaked in water or even certain chemicals, such as a brine solution.

The honey locust, *Gleditsia triacanthos*, has a granite-hard seed coat that not even the blows of a hammer can open. This attractive, delicately leaved landscape tree once had its seed capsules inadvertently left in a bucket of water by a horticulturist for over 15 years, yet the seed coat still

19

prevented water from entering to allow germination to take place.

Perhaps the super-hard seed casing of the honey locust is meant to protect the seeds inside from adverse environmental conditions in its native habitat. Without man's intervention, however, these seeds will break down naturally over the course of several years, thanks to microorganisms and chemical activities in the soil. Is it possible that the chances of seed survival and germination potential are increased when the opening of the seed capsules is spread out over several years?

VIABILITY

Many seeds can survive several years and still germinate and grow into healthy plants. This ability to develop and grow normally is often referred to as seed viability. Each plant species has its own seed-viability time frame, which varies widely from less than a year to many years. Seeds stored dry and at temperatures well below freezing seem to have the longest period of viability. At England's Millennium Seed Bank in Kew Gardens, seed is stored at $-4°F$. In 2002, the bank had 1.5 percent of the world's flora on deposit, about 4,000 species. These numbers are likely higher today.

The purplish-blue flowered Arctic lupine, *Lupinus arcticus*, found in the Arctic regions of North America can

Lupinus arcticus ssp. *subalpinus*, Arctic Lupine ALFRED COOK

grow even in rocky outcroppings and has been reported as having the longest period of seed viability known. In 1954, a mining engineer, working on placer mining operations in the Yukon Territory of northern Canada, exposed rodent burrows in a frozen silt face. This site contained several large, shiny black seeds of the Arctic lupine. Some of these seeds were collected and stored for a further 12 years before being sent to the National Museum of Canada. There, scientists selected the best-preserved seeds, those whose seed

21

Lupinus arcticus ssp. subalpinus BILL JEX

coats were as hard and shiny as that of freshly collected seed, and placed them on wet filter paper. Surprisingly, six of these seeds germinated within 48 hours. These were then placed in pots, and each grew normally, one even developing flowers after 11 months — something that does not usually take place until the third year of growth in the Arctic. After careful study, researchers discovered that the seed could not be less than 10,000 years old. (Visit the Canadian Museum of Nature website for the full story.)

In 2012, a group of Russian scientists found *Silene stenophylla* seeds buried in the Siberian permafrost and went on to grow them into flowering plants, though the seeds may have been around 30,000 years old. The seeds' age was determined by carbon dating, a means that some scientists feel may be inaccurate for this purpose, but it's clear that seed viability for several plant species is extraordinary.

22

DRIFTERS

Drifters are plants that rely on spreading their seed through the wind or floating on water. Both of these methods of seed dispersal can take the seeds considerable distances.

As children, many of us enjoyed blowing the light, feathery seeds of the dandelion and watching them float into the sky like so many tiny parachutes. Unwittingly we were aiding their already prolific reproduction methods. Though the dandelion is often considered a weed, an open field of their brilliant golden yellow flowers stretching as far as the eye can see is striking, particularly at dawn or dusk. Wind distributed seeds don't all rely on tiny parasols: the dust-like seeds of the orchid also allow the wind to carry them great distances.

Other seeds (and their capsules), like the coconut, *Cocos nucifera*, are dispersed by floating on the sea, often to ultimately inhabit some distant sandy seashore. Their seed capsules are buoyant, with a tough outer coat that allows them to travel great distances across the oceans.

HITCHHIKERS

Many plants are hitchhikers, their seed capsules catching a ride on a great diversity of wildlife, including humans, clinging to fur, feathers, skin or clothes. A few examples include the spiked fruits of *Tribulus orientalis* and *Pedalium*

23

Harpagophytum procumbens, grapple plant CITES SECRETARIAT

murex and the hooked fruits of *Bidens bipinnata* and *Scorpius muricatus*.

But the first plant that comes to mind here is the familiar weed burdock, *Arctium*. The fruits or seed cases of this plant have many hooks or burrs that clasp the fur of passing animals and the clothing of people who might brush by as well. The seeds can be carried many miles by this method, before they are knocked off by the carrier.

In an arid region of South Africa, the grapple plant, *Harpagophytum procumbens*, does something similar, though more aggressive, spreading out its snaky, leafy, branching stems into the sandy soil. The seed capsules have about 12 vicious arms, each with several sharp, strong hooks, pointing in different directions. Unfortunate wild animals often step on these cruel seedpods and the hooks become embedded in the sole of the animal's foot. After the poor creature endures many painful steps, the seed capsule finally breaks away and releases its seeds, much to the animal's relief.

24

Oenothera deltoides, birdcage plant, flowering in habitat JAMES M. ANDRÉ

Oenothera deltoides, birdcage plant, seed capsule GLENN AND MARTHA VARGAS
© CALIFORNIA ACADEMY OF SCIENCES

The *Proboscidea* species of the American west have long seed capsules with two lengthy hooks that easily fasten onto sheep wool. In this way, its seeds are spread considerable distances as the sheep search for greener pastures.

WANDERERS

Wanderers roam far and wide to find a suitable home, sometimes for themselves, but more often for their offspring. Their seeds are usually spread when their seed capsules are blown by the wind.

In the shifting desert sand dunes not far from coastal Oregon, the incredibly beautiful and fascinating birdcage

25

plant, *Oenothera deltoides*, bears many flowers, each an almost shimmering pinkish white with a yellowish throat.

Weeks after blossoming, a more amazing display takes place. Even though the birdcage has long roots, the shifting sands of the desert often expose them to the intensely hot sun, making them shrivel. The stems then curl upward and the plant forms a hollow latticed ball so different in appearance that it could almost be mistaken for another plant! The wind then rolls the birdcage across the landscape until it finds a more suitable place to distribute its seeds. The plant often travels many miles and days before coming to rest at the new home for its offspring.

Perhaps the best-known wanderer is that icon of Western ghost towns, the tumbleweed, or Russian thistle, *Salsola tragus* (syn. and often better known as *S. kali*). Annual herbs from a fibrous root system, these multi-branched plants are actually quite attractive in their youth, with their slightly spiky bluish-green foliage. As the season progresses, small clusters of purplish-pink flowers appear on the branches. By late summer, the plant's branches have become dry and hardened, and the plant assumes a ball-like shape. Then the whole plant breaks off from the roots at ground level, forming the well-known tumbleweed. Light and easily blown far and wide by the wind, the tumbleweed often traverses many miles, distributing its enormous quantities of seeds as it rolls across the land.

26

Another amazing wanderer can be found on the island of Crete, southeast of Greece. In this mostly flat, arid landscape, the Cretan plantain, *Plantago cretica*, starts as firm grasslike foliage with fluffy whitish flower clusters at the center. Later in the season, the seeds of this plant begin to ripen, and the stems curve out and downward, pushing against the soil with enough pressure to loosen its roots from the dry earth. The plant can literally pull itself out of the ground! Now ball-shaped, the plant rolls along with the wind to disperse its seeds.

Two further tumbleweed plants that, upon drying, form into a ball shape and are blown across the desert are both known as the resurrection plant. The first is also referred to as the Rose of Jericho, *Anastatica hierochuntica*; the second is *Selaginella lepidophylla*. If either of these plants encounters moisture in their travels, tumbling across the arid Middle Eastern landscape,

Salsola tragus (syn. S. kali), tumbleweed
JEAN PAWEK

it can root again in the new location where it can spread its stems and release its seeds. This ability to open and close with moisture and dryness is what has given both the name resurrection plant. Because of this evocative moniker, the plants are often sold as curiosities.

CATAPULTS *and* EXPLOSIVES

Hiking through a dense forest of tall Douglas fir trees near Pitt Meadows, in the southwest region of British Columbia, an unsuspecting person might hear loud popping and crackling sounds, like muffled firecrackers. If they got close enough, they might end up pelted with small black objects. This assault is the work of the Scotch broom, *Cytisus scoparius*, which disperses its seeds in late summer and early autumn. When ripe, the seed capsule stiffens and ejects its contents often considerable distances. Some seeds attach to the fur of animals or the clothing of humans as they pass by, becoming dispersed even farther.

In Mediterranean regions, such as the east coast of Italy, a tall relative of the common cucumber has a messier means of seed dispersal that gives it its common name, squirting cucumber. When the 2-inch fruit of *Ecballium elaterium* ripens, internal pressures cause the pods to explode with considerable force. This pressure, known as active ejection,

28

involves the uptake or loss of water within the pods. In this case, the ejection is wet and messy as the black seeds and their slimy pulp stream through the air as far as 20 feet. This explosive mechanism is set off by animals or people who brush against the plant and end up with some seeds and pulp as a souvenir of the encounter.

Ecballium elaterium, squirting cucumber DR. AMADEJ TRNKOCZY

Many other plants use catapult and explosive means of dispersing their seeds. Should you wish to investigate further, here are a few other examples.

Witch hazel, *Hamamelis virginiana*, found in the deciduous woods of eastern North America, also explosively catapults its seeds in autumn. The Brazilian rubber tree, *Hevea brasiliensis*, has seed capsules that, when ripe, explode violently, throwing their seeds great distances; and bear's breeches, *Acanthus mollis*, have seed capsules that burst loudly, throwing their seeds as if by

29

slingshot as far as 33 feet. The western corydalis, *Corydalis scouleri*, a wild plant found in wet, shady areas of western North America, has unusual flat seed capsules that detonate at the slightest touch, throwing their seeds far afield.

The parasitic dwarf mistletoe, *Arceuthobium*, uses explosive means to shoot its seeds up to 50 feet away and at a speed nearing 80 feet per second. The seeds of these

Hura crepitans, sandbox tree at Puentes Colgantes near Arenal Volcano, Costa Rica HANS HILLEWAERT/CC-BY-SA-4.0

mistletoes are coated with an extremely sticky substance that clings like glue to surfaces. Whenever moist weather arrives, these seeds germinate, often high up in the canopy of their main host plant, the ponderosa pine. In certain regions of western North America, these mistletoes can cause considerable damage to the pines.

Perhaps the most dramatic and noisiest plants with exploding seed capsules are the monkey's dinner bell or sandbox tree, *Hura crepitans*, in the rain forests of North and South America. When ripe, the seed capsules of these trees dry out and burst open, forcibly ejecting their seeds up to 40 feet.

PLANTS THAT PLANT THEIR OWN SEEDS

Some plants develop the ability to plant their own seeds. Sounds almost fanciful, but it's true.

In southern Crete, the annual stork's bill, *Erodium gruinum*, forms large violet-blue flowers in spring, then later in summer the flowers become seed capsules. When the seed ripens, it detaches itself from the capsule as if flung from a slingshot, and once it lands on the ground, it curls into a tight spiral. This twisting and curling enables the seed to drill into the soil, much like an auger. If you place a stork's bill seed on your hand, it will twist and untwist, like a corkscrew, as if it were trying to plant itself in your warm, moist palm.

31

Erodium cicutarium, seed capsule

The amazing seeds respond as well to the moisture in the air, and have even been used commercially in the manufacture of hygrometers, instruments that measure humidity in the atmosphere. Several other *Erodiums* behave similarly, including one, *E. cicutarium,* found in forested regions of western North America. *E. manescavii* is a lovely fern-leaved perennial species from the Pyrenees. Try growing one of these *Erodiums* in your garden, as children (and adults too) are fascinated to see the seeds dance in their palms.

Ivy-leaved toadflax, *Cymbalaria muralis* (syn. *Linaria cymbalaria*), native to the Mediterranean but widely found elsewhere, have trailing stems that root at the nodes and ivy-like leaves, and will grow on almost vertical rock. They bear numerous small lilac flowers, each with a yellow patch at the throat. The ivy-leaved toadflax raises its flower stalks

32

Cymbalaria muralis, ivy-leaved toadflax VIRGINIA SKILTON

from the stony wall, reaching toward the light. But, as soon as the flowers are fertilized, these same remarkable stalks curve in the totally opposite direction to deposit their seeds in the dark crevices of the rock wall.

The annual peanut plant, *Arachis hypogaea*, develops seedpods once its yellow flowers fade. Each pod is held by a

33

stalk, which gradually lengthens to grow down into the soil. Its seeds then ripen beneath the ground. Cyclamen also has stems that coil downward, bringing the seed capsule into contact with the soil. In effect, it too plants its own seeds.

Cyclamen JESSE VERNON TRAIL

CHAPTER THREE

VEGETATIVE REPRODUCTION

Though seeds are the main means that flowering plants use to reproduce, there are several other ways, depending on the plant species. These other methods are often referred to as vegetative reproduction and include runners, suckers, stolons, rhizomes, offsets, bulbs, corms and tubers. Some plants also have the remarkable ability to spread prolifically simply by way of detached pieces of stem, leaf or root. We will begin with their stories.

BITS *and* PIECES

A common weed in many lawns around the world, the slender speedwell, *Veronica filiformis*, is a hairy spring-blooming perennial. These plants creep through the grass by means of rhizomes and many slender stems, rooting at

35

Veronica filiformis, speedwell VIRGINIA SKILTON

the nodes, forming dense mats here and there. The saucer-shaped flowers are a light blue to lavender blue. This particular species of *Veronica* is especially remarkable since it almost never produces seeds, yet it still spreads rapidly when broken pieces split or detach easily from the parent plant or by its creeping rhizomes and rooting stems. This species can easily become invasive if conditions are to its

36

liking. For example, whenever we cut the grass with our lawn mowers, this weed is chopped into little pieces, each of which will readily root and start a new plant. Millions of individuals can come from one single plant, much to the chagrin of the homeowner.

A couple of other well-known plants that spread in a similar manner are the invasive Bishop's weed or goutweed, *Aegopodium podagraria*, and many of the low-growing, small-leaved species of garden sedum or stonecrop, though the latter is much better behaved and seldom weedy.

For a highly exemplary plant that spreads rapidly by its detached bits and pieces, to the point of extreme invasiveness, we need to go back in time to Australia between about 1839 and 1939. In 1839, a single plant of the prickly pear cactus species, *Opuntia stricta*, was brought into the country through Sydney and planted as a garden ornamental. No thought was given to its incredible ability to naturalize and inhabit the pastoral land. But proliferate it did, and quickly. Farmers tried to plow the plants under, but instead of reducing the number of this cacti, only produced many more plants instead. You see, the prickly pear cactus reproduces mainly when portions of its stem break off and root to start new plants — and it spreads with astonishing speed. Large portions of Queensland and eastern Australia became infested with the plants. They were estimated to

37

Opuntia streptacantha DANIEL L. NICKRENT

have first spread at the rate of about one million acres per year, and by 1925, nearly 25 million acres were overrun with prickly pear cactus.

Unfortunately, other species of prickly pear cactus, such as *O. vulgaris* and *O. ficus-indica*, had also been introduced into the Australian landscape. However, the infestation was eventually brought under biological control using the cochineal

38

insect and the cactoblastis moth. By 1934, 90 percent of the prickly pear cacti were eliminated by these methods.

There are other regions of the world where certain prickly pear cactus species became an invader, including Madagascar and parts of drier Mediterranean countries. For example, early in the twentieth century, *O. ficus-indica* and *O. stricta* had infested about 2.2 million acres of eastern South Africa's landscape; but again, the cochineal insect and cactoblastis moth brought the invasion under control.

Most if not all *Opuntia* species have fleshy succulent stem segments, joints or pads that are often brittle and easily detached simply by touching; hence the bits and pieces that spread new plants so prolifically. These pieces stick to the skin of animals and the skin and clothing of humans and are carried away, often to great distances, to start new plants in a new location. Most species also have sharp spines and often bear vividly colored flowers in hues of red or yellow. The green, yellow, red or orange fruits of many species are edible. They are striking, but several species have the potential to be highly invasive.

RUNNERS, SUCKERS, RHIZOMES *and* STOLONS

Runners, suckers, rhizomes and stolons are similar and very effective reproductive methods — so effective that they also can make a species invasive.

39

A runner is a horizontal stem that creeps along the surface of the ground and roots at the nodes to form new plants. The best known example is the strawberry. Suckers are similar to runners except that the horizontal stems are below the ground. Several of the sumacs, *Rhus* species, are examples. Rhizomes are thickened stems, more swollen than suckers, that creep on or below the soil surface. They contain stored food, and new roots can form from their underside. New plants develop from these, and so the plant spreads rapidly. Many perennials, such as ginger and rhizomatous iris, spread this way. A stolon is a slender, rapidly spreading rhizome, runner or creeping branch or stem that runs along the ground or just below the soil surface, developing new roots as it spreads. Many new plants are produced by this vegetative reproduction method.

Some stolons are submerged, and these will be explored when we discuss aquatic and marginally aquatic plants in Chapter 16. Two of these extremely invasive aquatic plants that spread by stolons are the water hyacinth, *Eichhornia crassipes*, with its exquisite flowers, and the water lettuce, *Pistia stratiotes*. The extensive mats of foliage these two plants produce clog many a waterway in tropical and subtropical regions. This choking growth can also cripple other submerged vegetation, and even fish and aquatic animals, by blocking sunlight and affecting water temperatures.

Imagine lush green foliage covering and swallowing up everything in sight, including cars, tractors, trees and even houses. It sounds like a scene from a science-fiction movie; but, believe it or not, in certain areas of the southern U.S. this is reality. The culprit vine is often aptly referred to as "the vine that ate the South," though it is more commonly known as kudzu, *Pueraria montana* var. *lobata*. Talk about invasive, this extremely fast-growing climber can grow up to 12 inches a day, and the plants send out underground roots or stems that can grow up to 30 new plants. The kudzu was originally introduced to the southern U.S. from Japan in the late 1800s, probably quite innocently as an ornamental vine. However, as of 2000, this clambering, aggressive vine was estimated to have engulfed well over 1.5 million acres.

OFFSETS, BULBS, CORMS *and* TUBERS

Offsets, bulbs, corms and tubers are often referred to as underground storage organs or geophytes. (Rhizomes are also often included as geophytes.)

An offset is a young plant that develops at or near the base of the parent plant. An excellent example is hens and chicks, *Sempervivum*.

Bulbs are essentially swollen underground food-storage organs or modified stems that produce their own roots at the base, such as onions, lilies, tulips, garlic and daffodils.

41

Next time you buy onions and garlic for cooking and eating, have a look at where the bulb roots are located. The swollen stem is the main edible part of these two vegetables.

Corms, common to plants like crocus, gladioli and many cyclamens, are swollen bulb-like underground stems.

Tubers are subterranean food-storage organs, important in the development of new plants in many species, such as the familiar potato, yam and sweet potato. Tubers are sometimes referred to as tuberous roots. Though by no means the largest, certain edible yams, *Dioscorea* species, can grow huge tubers of up to 100 pounds. Just one of these tubers would provide meals for many people. The only drawback might be that a tractor or excavator would be required to dig it up.

CHAPTER FOUR

GROWING CHALLENGES

THE VITAL IMPORTANCE *of* LIGHT

Virtually all plants need light to survive. To demonstrate this, all one needs to do is grow two plants of the same species, one in the dark and one in the light. The one grown in the light will develop normally, assuming all other life-giving requirements are present, whereas the one grown in the dark will become etiolated. The plant grown in the dark will stretch extensively, searching for the life-sustaining benefits only light can provide. Its stems become long and weak, with few tiny leaves, if any. This plant becomes white or yellowish, and its root system does not develop properly.

Have you ever observed weeds or grass trying to grow under a board or plank? Such plants are always discolored, with much longer stems than usual: they are etiolated.

This stretching for light is also observable in many plants growing in dense shade. You may have even seen plants whose growth occurs only on the one side where they receive sunlight. Light is also essential to many life-giving processes in plants, not least of which is photosynthesis.

WEATHER, CLIMATE *and* RELATED FACTORS

Imagine standing high on a mountain slope in the European Alps during a fiercely windy, bitterly cold winter's day. You shiver with the hope of relief, but none will come, for you are unable to move and shelter is nowhere to be found. Midsummer in another extreme climate amid the drifting sands of the arid Atacama Desert in Chile — the air is dry, the sun blistering and the landscape parched. This climate is, of course, what certain plants must endure — or, better still, adapt to.

These two examples address only some of the weather extremes certain plants experience, such as wind, heat and cold. Other plants, such as those in deserts or mountainous regions, may have to cope with extreme temperature fluctuations each and every day.

There are plants, including numerous bulbs, that survive periods of heat or cold simply by avoiding the sun's heat in summer and/or the bitter cold in winter. This is a type of dormancy — the state when a plant seems to completely

44

stop growing, and all other metabolic and physiological activities slow down significantly. With the majority of herbaceous perennials and bulbous plants, dormancy occurs when leaves and stems have died back to beneath ground level. These plants survive the adverse conditions as underground storage organs such as fibrous roots, tubers and rhizomes. Other plants, including many deciduous trees and shrubs, lose their foliage and enter the dormant state to avoid extreme cold or heat. In colder climates, even evergreens and conifers slow down their growth considerably during frigid winters, as a means to protect themselves.

One more striking example of weather-related environmental adaptation comes from the wet jungles of the Amazon Basin in central Brazil. There, even when there is not a torrential downpour or constant drizzle, the air is filled with a thick mist and the ground is moist or wet. Plants here seem to enjoy and thrive in these moist conditions.

We have addressed some of the main weather- and climate-related extremes that plants must endure and adapt to. But heat, cold, temperature fluctuations, wind and rain are not the only such factors that can threaten plant survival. Plants may also have to endure fire, solar radiation, intense sun exposure, air pollution and more. Other factors involved in plant survival include climate, topography, geology, freezing and thawing, altitude, latitude, humidity and short growing seasons. Photosynthesis and other physiological activities of plants can be strongly affected by environmental conditions.

ABOVEGROUND PERILS

Climate aside, some aboveground perils include lack of pollinators, lack of seed dispersers, seed viability and germination problems. In some instances, male plants or female plants may be scarce or nonexistent in a region, and reproduction may be impossible.

Then there are plant stresses, such as insect, fungal, bacterial and disease attacks. There are instances where one species of plant may take over the native habitat of another species. Other plants may even strangle a host plant.

Further aboveground perils that plants may face include mechanical damage, salt spray and lack of light, air or water.

BELOWGROUND HAZARDS

Roots and the soil they grow in are the main source of water, air and nutrients for plants; therefore, belowground conditions and hazards have a major impact on a plant's survival. While many plants have shown a remarkable ability to adapt to the soil in their native habitat, some of the soil adversities that plants may confront include

46

- shallow soil where root growth, water and nutrients are minimal;
- cracks and crevices to which certain plants have to cling for dear life;
- acid, alkaline or saline soils;
- polluted soils or soils with toxic levels of certain minerals and other elements;
- excessively moist or dry soils;
- lack of porosity or proper drainage, related to hardpan or clay soils with insufficient air for plant roots to breathe or take up water and nutrients;
- soils that are virtually devoid of nutrients or whose nutrients are unavailable for plant uptake;
- excessively rocky, sandy or clayish soils that can stymie root development;
- freezing and thawing of soil;
- depth of frost;
- depth of snow cover;
- soil temperature;
- insect, disease and animal attacks on roots;
- attacks from parasitic plants;
- lack of water, rainfall or any other sources of moisture.

47

As you can see, soil and how plants grow in soil is a book-length subject in itself. Here, our main purpose is to understand and become aware of the many soil and plant root challenges.

CHAPTER FIVE

THE VITAL IMPORTANCE OF WATER AND AIR

Water is not only the most abundant matter on earth, but it is also essential to all life on the planet. The vast, awesome oceans compose around 70 percent of the planet's surface. Beyond that, there are glaciers, ice caps, mist, fog, clouds and all forms of precipitation, such as rain and snow. Don't forget lakes, streams, groundwater, runoff and water in the soil. And there's more — the water in the bodies of all living organisms.

Water and air are intricately interrelated. When we speak of air here, we refer mainly to the oxygen and carbon dioxide portion. These two elements, like water, are essential to all life on earth, particularly in the plant processes of photosynthesis and respiration.

To begin, plants are composed of 85 to 90 percent water — a pretty phenomenal percentage. This water content is often found in plant leaves and particularly in herbaceous plants. The importance of water becomes evident when moisture is reduced by heat, drought or other means — if water loss is extreme, the plant will wilt and eventually die.

WATER ENTERS *the* PLANT

Most of the nutrients found in a plant enter through its roots, during exchanges with the soil. Other water enters the plant through the leaves, mostly in a gaseous exchange with the atmosphere. This is the complex biochemical pathway known as photosynthesis. Photosynthesis is essentially sunlight reacting with water and carbon dioxide to release oxygen and produce sugars and other nutrients for the plant's use. In other words, nutrients, including water, are transported both up and down the plant in a constant flow by photosynthesis and other physiological activities.

Submerged aquatic plants, such as species of *Elodea*, operate a bit differently, obtaining water directly through their epidermal cells. Some land plants, like the coastal redwoods of western California and certain coastal desert plants — including bromeliads in the Atacama Desert, the cloud forests of tropical regions and the wonder plant of the Namib Desert — absorb much or even all of their water, in the form of fog, mist or dew, through their foliage and stems.

50

There are two primary types of root systems: fibrous and taproot. Fibrous roots mostly grow in the portions of the soil close to the surface, whereas taproots send a strong main root deep into the ground to reach underground water sources. Because the roots are the plant's main source of water, it stands to reason that the more roots a plant has, the better its ability to take up water. Keep in mind, though, that other factors, such as soil structure and soil texture, also play a role.

Contrary to what many think, the aboveground portion of most plants is taller than its belowground roots are deep. Roots seldom go any further than 10 feet into the ground, regardless of the depth of well-drained soil. Even the roots of trees rarely grow much deeper than this. Many plants, including trees, send out their roots horizontally as well as — or instead of — going vertically. For certain plants, such as many cacti and desert plants, these horizontally spreading roots can reach as far as 60 feet from the plant's stem or trunk. The volume of a root system is usually as extensive as the aboveground portion of the same plant, and this applies to most trees as well.

On the northern coast of California, the majestic, awe-inspiring big trees *Sequoiadendron giganteum* and their close cousins the California redwoods, *Sequoia sempervirens*, are

51

considered to be the tallest in the world, with some specimens attaining lofty heights of 360 feet and even higher. The trees do not even begin to branch until 50 to 100 feet up the trunk, but the foliage cover is so dense that it prevents sunlight from reaching the forest floor, except in some scattered clearings. Each of these huge trees has a thick, fibrous, deeply furrowed bark of a strikingly beautiful reddish brown. The big trees are shorter-growing but wider, with individual specimens recorded at nearly 25 feet in diameter, at breast height.

Despite their height, their roots go only 4 to 6 feet into the ground; but their mostly fibrous root system spreads about 40 to 50 feet in all directions. The soil here is shallow, with a thick spongy layer of mulch at the base of the trees. These lofty trees relish the dense fog found on the Pacific Ocean coastline, which is a main source of their water.

Many of the tallest and best-known California redwoods and big trees have had fence barriers built around them to keep tourists from getting too close. After years of visitors trampling the soil surface, some of these trees were beginning to suffer suffocation of the roots due to the compaction of the surface soil.

THE SOIL, ROOTS, WATER *and* AIR CONNECTION

As most water is taken up by the plant through the roots, it is fitting that we delve deeper into understanding how the soil and plants work together. As you will see, water and air are intricately involved in this relationship.

Soil texture — its structure, permeability and porosity — is crucial to the soil-plant relationship. Soil texture refers to the size of soil particles and how they hold together. To better understand this, think of rocks, coarse and fine sand, clay or silt. The larger the soil particles, the more spaces for water and air; the smaller the soil particles, the fewer spaces. Water drains quickly in a coarse sand or rocky soil, whereas water drains, or is absorbed, much more slowly in a clay soil. Soil texture also affects the water-holding ability of the soil, and hence the availability of water for plant uptake. One can see, then, that soil texture is an important factor in water drainage and absorption, soil aeration and root growth. An ideal soil consists of 25 percent water and 25 percent air, with the rest being mostly minerals and organic matter. The best soils for root growth have a blend of particle sizes and pore spaces. The smaller soil particles are especially important for nutrient absorption by plant roots. Of course, the native habitat or environment of each type of plant strongly influences its adaptation to the soil.

Plant roots need air spaces in the soil to grow properly and to absorb water and nutrients. The oxygen component of this air is necessary for respiration, as well — all plant cells respire. If pore spaces are few, oxygen availability is

reduced and plant roots cannot grow. This suffocation can even occur when there is an abundance of water. For example, when a soil is saturated with water, plants can still suffer from a lack of water, because air is scarce. Also, in a saturated soil, when oxygen is deficient, carbon dioxide given off during respiration can accumulate to toxic levels. Of course, plants differ greatly in their tolerance to a water-saturated soil.

Air scarcity mostly occurs in soil containing a high percentage of clay. A soil can also be compacted by pressure, such as tractor ruts on a farmer's field or well-worn pathways on a hiking trail, often making it impossible for plant life to grow.

THE IMPORTANCE *of* WATER *to the* PLANT

Water plays a vital role in plant health, growth and survival in four main ways.

First, water helps to maintain a reasonably constant temperature in plants. It acts like the coolant in your car's radiator that keeps the car engine cooler than the air outside during a hot summer day. Transpiration — basically water evaporation from a plant — is similar to when we perspire to keep our bodies cooler. Over 90 percent of a plant's water loss is through its leaves, much of that through transpiration. Another way to put it: as the temperature rises in

54

summer heat, respiration increases and the plant may suffer water loss if there is not enough water in the soil.

Second, water is an excellent solvent, both in the soil solution for nutrient availability and in uptake within the plant. In fact, water is often referred to as the universal solvent because it dissolves so many chemicals, including salts. It affects such things as alkalinity and acidity of the soil.

Third, water acts as the transport system for nutrients and other chemicals throughout the plant, as well as enables chemical and physiological processes essential to plant life, such as photosynthesis and protein synthesis.

Finally, water maintains turgidity in plants. The less water there is within the plant, the more limp and wilted it becomes.

HEAT *and* DROUGHT TOLERANCE

When we speak of the vital importance of water and air to plants, we must also consider heat and drought tolerance, which are closely associated with the availability of water. Heat tolerance among plants is often associated with drought tolerance, but there are plants that are tolerant of heat but are not tolerant of drought, and vice versa.

Once the temperature reaches about 86°F, plant growth slows down dramatically or even ceases. Of course, this depends on the plant, as each has its own

55

temperature-tolerance range. The cactus, for example, can handle scorching heat of 122°F or even higher once fully established in its habitat. There is a report of one prickly pear cactus existing in the blistering heat of 156°F.

Many plants utilize more than one and often several heat- and drought-tolerance survival strategies.

LEAVES

Fine hairs help trap moisture to protect leaves from heat and drought. A couple of examples of such woolly species are many *Artemisia* and *Verbascum*. Silver, gray or blue foliage helps to reflect light and heat, whereas darker-colored foliage tends to absorb more of the sun's heat.

Some plants, such as certain bromeliads, trap moisture in their leaves. A few, including the compass plant, *Silphium laciniatum*, move or position their leaves to avoid the direct heat of the sun — only their leaf edges face its rays. Others, like Portulaca and certain sedums, have small succulent leaves that grow densely to shelter the roots. Southern Africa's *Pachypodium rosulatum*, for example, looks like a shrubby boulder covered with short succulent leaves. Truly alien-looking plants!

Other leaf-surface-reduction adaptations to help to retain water include the needle-like foliage of *Armeria* and *Pinus*; the scale-like foliage of certain junipers; leathery foliage; and filigree foliage, such as that of several *Achillea* species and the California poppy. The spines of cacti are actually modified leaves and, as such, reduce the total surface area (somewhat like needle foliage), thereby helping to reduce moisture loss from the plant in heat and drought. Some plants, including many legumes, curl or fold up their leaves during the heat of the day. Others, such as the tree spurge, *Euphorbia dendroides*, do without leaves, shedding them during the summer.

Many evergreen plants — several needle-leaved conifers, small-leaved plants like Portulaca, sedums and more — have leaves that are coated with a thick waxy cuticle that helps retain moisture and resists the dehydrating effect of the sun's intense heat. The thicker this cuticle layer, the less dehydration occurs.

STEMS *and* TRUNKS

To endure long periods of heat and drought, many plants have large water reservoirs, such as swollen trunks. Columnar and barrel cactus species store an enormous volume of water in their stems. These cacti can survive prolonged periods of drought — from several months to several years. In southwest Africa, for example, one species of tree is such a good reservoir it earned the common name flask tree, *Moringa ovalifolia*.

In the dry forests of eastern Brazil lives a strange tree that seems like something out of a science-fiction novel. This

57

relatively rare and little-known species of *Cavanillesia* is close to the epitome of distortion for a tree. Rather than being bottle-like in appearance, it looks more like an enormous turnip. Its egg-shaped trunk is almost three times taller than it is wide and its narrow base consists of a small cluster of surface roots. The trunk curves with a greatly enlarged middle portion, narrowing up into a sparse, mostly horizontal,

Pachypodium rosulatum gracilius in the Isalo National Park, Madagascar
BERNARD GAGNON/CC-BY-SA 3.0, 2.5, 2.0. 1.0

Moringa drouhardii, bottle tree GERALD AND BUFF CORSI © CALIFORNIA ACADEMY OF SCIENCES

scrawny branching crown. The eastern Brazilian region is also home to several of the similar but much more common pot belly trees, *Cavanillesia arborea*. These trees can vary considerably in the degree of distortion of their trunks, branches and crowns, likely as a response to the environmental conditions each specimen endures. The common feature in all these trees is the trunk's swollen midsection, which stores a great deal of water.

Madagascar is home to a genus of particularly notable succulent plants, *Pachypodium*. *Pachypodium* often have swollen trunks and unique shapes to deal with their often harsh, dry environment. Elephant's foot, *P. geayi*, is a tall, thorny, bottle-shaped bush with grayish-white bark and a fringe of branches at the top.

Another plant native to Madagascar, *M. drouhardii*, relies on a swollen trunk as well. These trees are attractive

59

in their own way, with their bloated bright white trunks, sparse branching and feathery foliage.

In exceptionally dry areas of South Africa and nearby Namibia, *Cyphostemma juttae* is a very fat succulent, with tufts of leafy branches at the top and peeling brownish-yellow bark. Not a pretty plant, but fascinating!

Cyphostemma juttae JAMES M. CARPENTER

ROOTS

Plants with dense, fibrous root systems are able to soak up moisture like a sponge. Cacti and many desert perennials, for example, have extensive shallow root systems to capture as much moisture and nutrients as they can from close to the soil surface after the infrequent rainfall that occurs in the desert. The roots of many Australian *Banksia* and South African *Protea* species have similar root systems.

In the hot, arid savannah of southern Africa, the grotesquely fat yet utterly fascinating baobab species, *Adansonia digitata*, endures drought with an extensive horizontal root system that may spread up to 330 feet around the tree. In the Sudan and elsewhere, the hollowed trunk is used as a water reservoir. The branching of this tree is also stout, often with sparse leafing at the ends. In Queensland, Australia, the similar

Adansonia digitata, baobab JIM ADAMS

Adansonia grandidieri, Madagascar baobab

A. gregorii grows to similar proportions, whereas Madagascar's *A. grandidieri* is almost uniformly fat up the length of its trunk.

Many cacti, as well as other plants (such as Tree of Heaven, *Ailanthus*), spread their roots far and wide to increase their potential to find and absorb water.

Plants with deep taproots or simply deep roots, such as many legumes (including rye) and lupines, are able to reach groundwater far below the surface, while plants such as yams, sweet potatoes and day-lilies have plump, swollen roots in which to store water.

GROWTH HABITS *and* ENVIRONMENTAL ADAPTATIONS

Desert annuals avoid heat and drought by simply existing as seeds for much of the year. Other plants, including many bulbs, avoid these adverse conditions by going dormant in summer.

Some plants grow flat to the ground in dense mats, to shield their roots from the hot summer sun, while others, such as many alpines and Mediterranean-climate plants, are able to penetrate deep into cracks and crevices found in rocky, mountainous habitats for shelter.

CHAPTER SIX
THE ARCTIC EXAMPLE

When we think of the Arctic, images of a vast, desolate landscape often come to mind. Bitter cold permeates the air throughout much of the year, often accompanied by incessant winds. But with the sunshine and warmth of an Arctic spring and summer, many areas of this stark region become alive with the colorful flowers of plants like moss saxifrage, Arctic poppy and Arctic willow herb. Most of these stalwart flowering plants hug the ground in a loose to dense carpet. Here and there, taller, colorful blooming plants and tough conifers can be found, particularly where they are protected from the winds by, say, a mound of soil or a rock.

There are several different ways to define the Arctic, but for our purposes we will take it to mean the frigid area north

64

of the natural tree line and within the Arctic Circle. The tree line is the farthest north that trees can grow. Beyond this is the tundra, where most of the Arctic lies. Any trees that are able to grow in the tundra are few and far between, and they are increasingly dwarfed and gnarled the further north you go because of nearly constant winds that blow unimpeded across the virtually flat landscape.

Most of the Arctic tundra can be considered a polar desert. Arctic drought is a major concern, which means Arctic plants must find ways to conserve vital moisture. To put things into perspective, the tundra rarely has a month above 50°F, and annual precipitation is low, at less than 10 inches per year in most areas. Coastal regions are generally warmer and wetter, moderated by oceanic influences, allowing for more abundant and even lush plant growth compared to the drier interior areas. Greater plant growth can also be found in lowlands and sheltered valleys and on the banks of streams and rivers. In these areas, early summer melting of the top layer of permafrost often makes the soil soggy. This moisture is of immense importance for the growth of the plants in these regions.

Plant life in the tundra is either widely dispersed or huddled together in groups. Dwarf shrubs, sedges, grasses, mosses and lichens are the predominant vegetation, and all grow relatively close to the ground. Even in such an

65

inhospitable environment, there are about 1,700 plant species, including 400 or more flowering plant species. Several are exceptionally beautiful.

The majority of these Arctic plant species are perennial, because the growing season is too brief for most other plants. Growth is also often slow because of the adverse conditions in the Arctic; nearly all tundra plants are long-lived. The few annuals found in the Arctic remain as seeds through the cold winter months, then germinate and grow quickly once spring arrives.

Because the Arctic climate is characterized by bitter cold, often accompanied by relentless drying winds, and because the soil there is shallow and nutrient deficient, it is difficult for plants to root and establish themselves. Permafrost is often found only inches from the soil's surface. On top of all these adversities, Arctic plants also have a fleeting growing season. They must grow, develop and produce seeds within a period of just a few months. Some plants, such as the purple saxifrage, *Saxifraga oppositifolia*, get a jump start by beginning to grow as soon as the sun appears in early spring and a shallow layer of snow and frozen soil begins to thaw. This growth often develops from stem or flower buds that were formed at the end of the previous growing season. Another excellent example here is the woolly lousewort, *Pedicularis lanata*, a pretty little plant

66

that produces thick-skinned buds that remain in the ground throughout the winter, until spring arrives.

When spring does come to the Arctic, the sun shines both day and night for almost six months. In June and July, the sun just dips down to the horizon and then rises again, providing 20 to even 24 hours of sunlight per day. Unfortunately, it takes some time before the spring sun is warm enough to initiate plant growth. Then, after the short growing season, bitterly cold winter temperatures again arrive, all too early, accompanied by six months or more of darkness.

On a positive note, there are no hurricanes, tornadoes or even thunderstorms in the Arctic tundra. Also, solar radiation is less intense because it travels a longer distance through the atmosphere and is spread across a larger surface. That said, because of global warming and ozone depletion, ultraviolet radiation in the Arctic is increasing. Many Arctic plants have thick leaves and protective pigments to help shield them from these added adversities.

All plant cells have a high water content that is at great risk of freezing in frigid climates. To combat this, some Arctic plants have ways to insulate their cells and reduce their water content, including complex chemical processes that serve as a form of antifreeze. The optimum temperature for most Arctic or alpine plants to grow is around $50°F$ to $68°F$, but several plant species in the Arctic have

tissues that can survive temperatures well below freezing, up to −58°F, without permanent injury. For example, the Dahurian larch, *Larix gmelinii* (syn. *L. dahurica*), grows close to the Arctic tree line, in the coldest, northernmost forest of all, the Kolyma region of northwest Siberia. This tough deciduous conifer can tolerate extremely cold temperatures that would kill most other trees.

In comparison, other plants, including many conifers and deciduous plants of more temperate winter climates, also have complex chemical processes that serve as a form of antifreeze. However, the optimum temperatures for plants in temperate and even tropical regions are near 77°F to 86°F. The difference between tropical and temperate survival is that tropical plants will not tolerate the extremes in temperature to which the most temperate climate plants are often exposed.

These optimum temperatures for all plants vary not only from one species to the next, but also from one stage of development to the next, from one organ to the next and even from one metabolic activity to the next.

Now that we have a better understanding of the scientific factors for plants living in the Arctic, let us journey around the world to discover and appreciate many of these special Arctic plants, their attributes and adaptations.

HUGGING *and* HUDDLING

Two of the most prominent survival strategies of Arctic plants are growing close to the ground and huddling together. Both adaptations help to protect plants from the bitter cold and relentless winds.

The early-spring Arctic air is still briskly cold, and after the long, dark winter, the twenty-four hours of spring sunshine bring not only warmth, but also new life and color to the landscape as well. The grandeur and vast space is awe-inspiring.

The purple saxifrage is one of the first plants to bloom, with a beautiful, abundant display of brilliant magenta to bright pink-purple blossoms. Many of these plants become almost smothered by their large flowers. Some plants are loners on rock faces, in crevices, among stones and rocks or on flat tundra fields, providing striking beauty in an otherwise barren scene. Others are found in small groups in similar habitats. It is a sheer delight to come across vast carpets of these dense, thickly mounding plants.

Because of its ability to confront and even flourish in the face of adversity, the species has an extensive range in the upper Northern Hemisphere, including high in the Alps and the Rocky Mountains alpine tundra, as well as the Arctic tundra. An exceptionally tough plant, it is one of the four

Saxifraga oppositifolia, purple saxifrage DR. AMADEJ TRNKOCZY

northernmost flowering plants in the world, with specimens found growing on the north coast of Greenland.

The soil in the purple saxifrage's habitat is most often dry, gravelly to rocky, with the plants growing in the shallow layer above the permafrost. A ground-hugging perennial spread by trailing stems, the plant forms dense cushions and often huddles with other plants to keep even warmer. The

70

stems are tightly packed together, surrounded for the most part by tiny, rounded, leathery, overlapping, succulent evergreen and hairy-edged leaves, which are flat to catch maximum sunlight. Each of these features provides additional protection against the often cold and drying winds. This striking species would make a highly attractive rock-garden plant, though it has proven difficult to cultivate in warmer climates. Perhaps the purple saxifrage *prefers* adversity?

A little later in the spring, the Arctic locale unveils another perennial ground-hugger: moss campion, *Silene acaulis*. This delightful perennial also forms a densely packed mound of tiny leathery leaves and hugs the ground for warmth. In fact, the temperature within the plant can be 59°F warmer than the surrounding air — quite a difference! Growing from a woody taproot, which can penetrate deep into rock crevices for moisture, and a branched stem base, the plants form thick, dense cushions with abundant star-shaped bright pink to lavender single flowers hugging tightly to the cushion of foliage. There are a few varieties of this pretty little plant, each a perfect illustration of adaptation to the fierce, drying winds high in the Arctic. The success of its adaptations is further demonstrated by the broad distribution of moss campion throughout the Northern Hemisphere. It is not unusual to see many plant hummocks of moss campion snuggling together, forming

71

Silene acaulis, moss campion IAN GARDINER

an extensive carpet of vivid pink flowers that practically smother the plants. Where the foliage shows through, it appears much like patches of rich green moss.

Moving from the tundra's flatlands to a chain of tumbling streams and rugged mountains, we might find dwarf fireweed, *Epilobium latifolium* (syn. *Chamerion latifolium*), plants brightening the stark rocks. Somehow, each of these little plants holds on by finding moisture and nutrients in the highly visible rock crevices. It's a seemingly meager existence, but the dwarf fireweed still flourishes, spreading rapidly by its creeping rhizomes. Though the plants can grow a bit taller in more southerly locales, in the Arctic they are predominantly ground-huggers. Also known as dwarf willow herb, mainly because of its willow-like leaves, it is not related to the willows at all. You may be familiar with the closely related fireweed, *E. angustifolium*, which grows prolifically in the South,

Silene acaulis, moss campion DR. AMADEJ TRNKOCZY

especially after forest fires. The dwarf fireweed can also be found covering huge expanses of land in the Arctic, its bright pink or purplish-blue flowers providing color in an otherwise drab landscape. The plant is exceptionally tough, with specimens growing as far north as upper Ellesmere Island. Its main means of surviving such harsh, inhospitable conditions is by its ground-hugging habit and trailing, anchoring stems.

73

Chamerion latifolium,
dwarf fireweed ALFRED COOK

Even dwarf shrubs such as the Arctic willow, *Salix arctica*, can be found growing way up on the north portion of Ellesmere Island and on Banks Island, both part of the Canadian Arctic Archipelago. In more southern areas, the Arctic willow can grow a bit taller, but never higher than 10 inches. At higher latitudes, it mostly creeps along the ground, usually less than 4 inches high, with plants often found growing in thickets (or huddling together to keep warmer). Its long trailing branches root where they touch the soil's surface, thus ensuring the continuation of the species. Virtually all parts of the plant are covered with soft, silky, silvery hairs as extra protection from the often harsh environment.

It may sound like a joke, but the Arctic willow, despite its stature, has been called the largest "tree" in the high Arctic. This is because it is the northernmost woody plant in the world. It is also extremely slow-growing and very long-lived. One recorded specimen in eastern Greenland was found to be 236 years old. This amazing plant can grow in wet to dry areas with equal vigor. It's also quite striking, with white to reddish flower spikes or fluffy tufts, fuzzy male catkins (flowering spikes) and shiny green willow foliage that even turns bright red in the Arctic autumn.

Salix arctica, Arctic willow VIRGINIA SKILTON

Cassiope tetragona, Arctic mountain heather ALFRED COOK

Another huddling wonder can be found in north Alaska and the Yukon Territory. The white Arctic mountain heather, *Cassiope tetragona*, grows both on open rocky areas and moist to dry meadows, but it is most often found huddled together in groups, on moister sites where there is protection from wind as well. Just as lovely as its garden-heather cousins, this pretty little evergreen shrub

76

hugs the ground, forming dense mats consisting of leathery, finely haired, almost scale-like leaves. These cushions are packed together so tightly that the many kinds of insects that visit the plants experience almost subtropical conditions. Each nodding stem is topped by a single white to pinkish upside-down-bell-shaped flower. These are produced in profusion throughout the growing season. Arctic heather spreads by fibrous roots that form along its mostly prostrate stems.

There are many other ground-hugging and huddling flowering plants in the Arctic, but we will briefly address only one more here. Cottongrass, *Eriophorum angustifolium*, is a member of the sedge family (*Cyperaceae*), with a widespread distribution in the Northern Hemisphere, especially in more northerly regions. It spreads by ground-level or underground stems, often covering extensive areas of mainly moist to wet tundra with its cotton-like white inflorescences.

Eriophorum species, cottongrass
DR. AMADEJ TRNKOCZY

Mosses and lichens are also plentiful in the Arctic and should be considered here, even though our main focus is flowering plants. Lichen is both a fungus and an algae in symbiotic association. These soft-textured plants have no roots and form spongy cushions or mats and can even grow on bare rock. Without flowers or seeds, they reproduce by spores. Both lichens and mosses prefer shady locations, such as behind rocks.

WOOLLY COVERS

When it is cold and windy outside, we put on a warm sweater and a jacket. Many plants in the Arctic also wear a sort of woolly jacket. Woolliness or hairiness not only keeps plants warm, but also helps to reduce moisture loss. The degree of hairiness can range from fine and short to dense and long, practically covering the plant. Plants can have woolly stems, leaves, buds and even flowers.

In the Canadian Arctic Archipelago and much of the Northern Hemisphere grows a plant that is truly woolly, particularly in its early stages of growth when practically the whole plant, including the leaves, stems and flower heads, is covered with translucent hairs. Even the mature bright yellow daisy flower heads are surrounded at their bases by dense and translucent woolliness, which only adds to the plant's appeal. This abundant hairiness creates a kind of greenhouse effect,

78

Tephroserus palustris, mastodon flower, marsh fleabane ALFRED COOK

helping to prevent absorbed heat from escaping into the cold surrounding air. This special plant is known as both the mastodon flower and marsh fleabane, *Senecio congestus* (syn. *Tephroseris palustris*).

The mastodon flower is one of the rare annual plant species in the Arctic. Although its distribution is widespread in the Arctic and much of the upper Northern Hemisphere, it is actually a red-listed plant — a threatened, endangered or rare species — in many regions. It is mostly found in moist areas, such as stream banks, ponds and marshes.

The woolly or Arctic lousewort, another very hairy perennial, is one of the earliest spring flowers of the tundra. The intriguing early growth of the Arctic lousewort can be likened to a small ball of cotton. This dense woolliness traps the warmth from the early spring sun so that rapid flowering is encouraged. Under the protection of this

79

woolly cover, plants can be up to 25°F warmer than the air around them. As growth progresses, beautiful pink to purplish flowers seem to burst forth from the cottony mass, practically covering the plant at maturity. Dense and woolly hairs peek out from between the flowers and the stems are also densely woolly. Its softly hairy basal leaves are deeply divided and highly attractive. Established plants retain older and dead leaves at the base for extra protection from wind and cold.

The Arctic lousewort has a thick taproot, yet, as with other members of its genus, it is a root parasite on the roots of a host plant, such as certain grasses. The plants often grow in areas that are covered with snow in the winter, affording them additional protection from their harsh environment. Preferring dry, well-drained soils, this fascinating plant is found throughout much of the upper Northern Hemisphere.

Pedicularis lanata, Arctic lousewort
IAN GARDINER

LEAVES

We have already discussed how woolly hairs help protect plants from the rigors of their Arctic environment. Many other plants in the Arctic have thick leathery evergreen leaves with a juicy or succulent nature and a waxy coating. Each of these features helps plants retain moisture.

Autumn arrives all too early in the Arctic, but with it comes beautiful color on the foliage of two *Vaccinium* species. Most of us make use of the cultivated cranberry at festive times of the year, such as Thanksgiving, but did you know that the mountain cranberry — or lingonberry, as it is known by our Scandinavian friends — *Vaccinium vitis-idaea*, can be used in most of the same ways as the commercial variety and has a similar flavor? Some would say that because the lingonberry grows wild, its flavor is even better. This low, carpeting evergreen shrub spreads by underground rhizomes. It has white flowers

Pedicularis lanata, Arctic lousewort IAN GARDINER

81

Vaccinium vitis-idaea, lingonberry
DR. AMADEJ TRNKOCZY

followed by edible bright red berries, and its small, leathery green leaves turn purplish red to brilliant red in late summer and fall. Non-evergreen plants must take the time and energy to produce new leaves each year, whereas evergreens such as the lingonberry can devote their full attention to other metabolic activities during the short growing season. Both the evergreen leaves and their changing to red in autumn help the lingonberry utilize the lower light levels for photosynthesis. Our specimens are enjoying a moist part of the tundra, but keep in mind that the plants on the whole are quite adaptive, even to drier areas.

Another *Vaccinium*, the Arctic blueberry, *Vaccinium uliginosum*, is a low deciduous shrub that spreads by roots that develop along the trailing stems. It bears upside-down-bell-shaped pinkish-white flowers and wonderfully tasty dark blue to blackish edible berries. In autumn, the Arctic

82

blueberry carpets the landscape with its vivid red foliage, which, like the lingonberry, allows the plants to absorb more sunlight across a broader spectrum at a time when light in the north is beginning to wane. This changing of foliage color late in the season is characteristic of several other Arctic plants. Fall colors can range from reds and yellows to browns and rusts, and some Arctic species retain darker-colored foliage throughout the growing season to absorb more heat.

Leaf shape can offer cold protection as well. The leaves of the purple saxifrage, as discussed earlier, are small, ever-green, succulent and flat to catch maximum sunlight. They grow close together and have long hairs on the edges of each leaf for additional protection from wind and cold. The leaves of several species, like *Dryas*, have edges that roll under so that they touch or almost touch. Tight-clustering, overlap-ping, rolling under and small leaves are all adaptations to protect Arctic plants from bitter cold and strong winds.

DEAD FOLIAGE *as* PROTECTION

Many tundra plants retain their dead leaves rather than shed them each autumn. These dry leaves act as a mulch to protect the plant and next spring's buds from the frigid, drying winds of the Arctic. The dwarf fireweed is one plant that allows its leaves and stems to die during the winter, yet they remain on the plant until the following spring. Other

83

Dryopteris fragrans,
fragrant wood fern ALFRED COOK

species, such as thrift, *Armeria maritima*, have older leaves that die with the onset of winter, yet remain to protect the younger green foliage in the center of the plant.

The Canadian Arctic is also home to a unique plant, the fragrant wood fern, *Dryopteris fragrans*. It is the only fern that has its old, brown and dead foliage persist as a clump at its base, thus providing its own thick winter mulch as protection from arctic cold and wind. Also unusual for a fern, its younger central leaves remain evergreen, and its foliage is aromatic when handled. The leaves or fronds are leathery, with dense, papery scales and thick surface hairs — again, found only in this species of fern. The plants are rhizomatous or stoloniferous, often with a thick underground stem. Found throughout the upper part of the Northern Hemisphere, on slopes, ridges, cliffs and rock scree, it prefers dry, shaded, well-drained sites.

ROOTS, UNDERGROUND *and* UNDER SNOW

In spring in the tundra, the frozen top layer of soil thaws over the course of only three to four months, allowing roots to grow. Coastal areas, lowland sheltered valleys and the banks of rivers and streams often remain moist during the growing season, yet the soil remains shallow. In the drier interior areas, however, the situation can be considerably worse: such regions may be described as polar deserts. Here, the wind blows often unimpeded and can quickly dry the top layer of non-permafrost soil. Where snow does accumulate, it acts as a protective blanket for the plants during the long eight- to nine-month period before spring thaw arrives. Most of the snowfall occurs during the winter and predominantly in coastal areas or in drifts against rock and soil outcroppings.

Plants in the Arctic often have well-developed root systems for food and water storage during the lengthy winter (some of these plants can be food and water for us as well, if we are ever stranded in the Arctic). It has been said that Arctic plants are like icebergs: much more of the plant grows underground than above. This is true for many species that have extensive fibrous roots much longer than the aboveground plant growth, such as the Arctic sedge, *Carex fuliginosa*. Many plants have underground structures to store food and water, including the tubers of *Primula* species

85

and the rhizomes of the narrow reed grass, *Calamagrostis neglecta*. Such root structures allow Arctic plants to survive the frigid winters of the tundra.

FOLLOW *the* SUN

A rare and fascinating attribute of two plants found in the far north is the ability of their cup-shaped flowers to always face and follow the sun's path across the sky. These plants can absorb a great deal of the sun's warmth during the brief Arctic summers, raising their internal temperatures by several degrees. As a result, the flowers are warmer than the air around them. Flowers with this adaptation are usually yellow or white, because these colors better reflect heat into the flower. Also, the central disc of the flower is darker to absorb more of the sun's warmth. They are natural solar collectors!

Seeds developing deep inside the flowers mature quickly in this cozy abode. Insects also enjoy the warmth of these flowers, so pollination prospects are greatly enhanced. The tendency to turn toward the sunlight is known as positive heliotropism, a feature found in a handful of other plants, like the familiar sunflower.

The Arctic poppy, *Papaver radicatum*, grows both alone and in small groups. It seems to prefer moist, gravelly ground on the tundra flats. No one can deny that this is an absolutely exquisite plant, especially with its bright sulfur to soft yellow flowers, though at certain sites the flowers may be white or pinkish. The plant gives the impression of delicacy, but it is actually rugged in its harsh environment.

Papaver radicatum, Arctic poppy VIRGINIA SKILTON

The deeply dissected and softly furry gray to blue-green foliage of the Arctic poppy is delicate and attractive. Its tiny hairs and its stems help prevent damage from wet and cold. The foliage grows tightly together to form dense mounds, hugging the ground for further warmth, with the solitary flower stalks rising above, topped by the shell-like flowers that are always turned to face the sun. The Arctic poppy is circumpolar, with a wide distribution that also encompasses the southeast Greenland coast, north Alaska and the Yukon.

Mountain avens, *Dryas integrifolia*, is another heliotropic ground-hugging shrub that has intertwining stems that can spread to form extensive carpets. The plants grow

87

Dryas integrifolia, mountain avens ALFRED COOK

in tight buns and are virtually covered with hairs, including on the calyx, flowering stems and fruit capsules. The small green leaves are leathery evergreen, with most of the hair on the underside. Flower buds begin maroon colored, while the flowers are usually creamy yellow and sometimes white — daisy-like with a dark yellow central zone. Even the seed heads of the mountain avens are lovely — fluffy and soft despite their harsh surroundings.

CHAPTER SEVEN
ALPINE ADAPTATIONS

One of the most exquisite sights in nature is an alpine meadow in full bloom. In spring, the rolling, rocky, mountainous terrain is virtually carpeted as far as the eye can see with a great variety of brilliantly multicolored flowers. Yet these flowers are far from delicate, and many alpine plants require survival strategies similar to Arctic plants. The main difference is that Arctic plants grow in higher latitudes (the far north), whereas alpine plants grow in higher altitudes (mountains). Generally, both Arctic and alpine plants grow above the tree line, and both endure cold weather and often windy conditions for much of the year.

The two also share similar environmental adaptations: often dense, tight low-growth; hugging and huddling

89

together; woolliness or hairiness; small, thick, waxy or leathery leaves; dead foliage as protection; roots kept warm underground and under snow; and flowers that follow the sun for warmth. Some of these adaptations are also similar to those of desert plants (mainly the strategies for reducing water loss).

Because of the plants' similarities, a number of Arctic plants are also found in alpine areas as well, and many alpine plants grow in Arctic regions. A good example here is the lovely moss campion, which was discussed in the last chapter. Of course, many alpine plants are found only in specific alpine locations or environments.

Alpine regions are most often associated with high snow-covered mountain peaks. Although there are plants that live in such environments, alpine plants also inhabit rocky, seemingly barren sites, such as sheer cliffs and boulders, as well as grassy alpine meadows, and even woodland and boggy regions of the world's mountain ranges.

Since many alpine plants grow in areas where a deep layer of snow blankets them for the winter months, snow is essential for their survival, providing moisture and a protective layer of insulation from the bitter cold of winter. However, beneath a thick layer of snow, plants often suffer from drought because all the water is frozen and therefore

90

unavailable. Several species of alpines have adapted to this by going into winter dormancy. In spring, when the snow melts, abundant water is again available and growth resumes.

Many species of alpines have adapted to, endure and even flourish in their often rocky environment, which can include minimal soil, drying winds, a short growing season and large fluctuations in daily temperatures. As the elevation above sea level increases, so do sunlight and ultraviolet radiation.

High in the Andes Mountain range on the volcanic slopes of the Western Cordillera in southwest Bolivia, the *Polylepis*, a special genus of trees and shrubs, is native only to this rugged mountain terrain. These often gnarled and weather-beaten plants are scattered in sparse stands. In bold defiance of the harsh winds that sweep through these mountains, these stalwart plants extend their branches, bending and contorting to endure winds in a sort of regal determination to survive. Their multilayered, peeling, papery, mostly cinnamon-colored bark and delicate feathery foliage give the *Polylepis* pleasing beauty and charm for such tough plants.

Climbing even higher up the Andes reveals *Polylepis tarapacana*, a species that holds the world record for a

91

Polylepis species ROBERT F. NORRIS

woody plant growing at the highest altitude. It is likely the only tree in the world that can grow at altitudes of up to 17,060 feet — whereas trees more commonly grow at 12,000 to 13,000 feet above sea level.

In a rocky area of the Southern Alps, the gorgeous *Eritrichium nanum*, known as King of the Alps, grows in the

92

Eritrichium nanum, King of the Alps DR. AMADEJ TRNKOCZY

crevices and dips of the sloping cliffs. Each plant is a low, softly hairy, blue-green cushion of dense foliage covered with small yellow-centered and soft blue flowers. Where growing conditions are more favorable, a looser form of this same plant is found way over in the Rocky Mountains of North America.

93

Gentiana clusii, trumpet gentian DR. AMADEJ TRNKOCZY

In the same rocky cliffs, the trumpet gentian, *Gentiana clusii*, can be identified by a low, tight rosette of leathery bright green leaves that grow many solitary trumpet-shaped deep azure flowers with a paler eye. Fairies' thimbles, *Campanula cochleariifolia*, can also be found in cliff crevices. The dainty trumpet-shaped bright blue to violet-blue nodding flowers are low-growing treasures of the high Alps.

94

Campanula cochleariifolia, fairies' thimbles DR. AMADEJ TRNKOCZY

We have encountered only a small selection of the great number of beautiful alpine plants found growing in the high altitudes of mountainous regions around the world. For every alpine plant you look at, keep in mind how they adapted to their often cold and windy mountain environment.

CHAPTER EIGHT

LESSONS FROM THE DESERT

Often appearing barren and almost desolate, deserts are associated with sand, rock, dunes, hills, more sand and, infrequently, low, rugged mountains.

Some may be surprised that deserts or desert-like conditions prevail over 20 percent of the earth's land mass, and if you check environmental reports, desert conditions are actually increasing in many regions of the world. There are even parts of the Arctic that are known as polar deserts.

A desert, although generally considered a region with very little to no rainfall and scorching heat from the sun, may also have daily extremes of heat and cold, as well as strong, abrasive winds. Rainfall on a true desert usually measures less than 4 inches a year, though many desert regions experience about 8 inches or less annually. Rainfall, when it does occur on the desert landscape, typically comes in brief but torrential downpours, though it can be intermittent with long time-lapses between rains. With this little rainfall, desert air usually has very low moisture content, which only serves to intensify the aridity of deserts.

Life in desert regions also endures intense sunshine in the form of heat and solar radiation, plus greater daily temperature fluctuations than on any other type of landscape on earth. Whenever strong winds sweep across the desert — and this can be frequent or even constant in some areas — they drive sand and grit nearly horizontally. In some of these areas, the wind can turn into major dust storms and sandstorms. These winds can also shape beautiful sand dunes, as well as erode rock. The intricate designs they etch onto a desert landscape can be breathtaking.

In coastal deserts, the principal and sometimes only source of precious life-sustaining moisture comes from the fog that drifts in from cold offshore ocean currents. Loma are similar, but they encompass the infrequent, isolated mountains or steep coastal slopes of certain deserts that are often enveloped in a thick mist or clouds.

Plant life is frequently or seasonally sparse in these regions, yet deserts are home to some of the most remarkable and beautiful plants on earth. To endure the harsh environmental extremes of their home, desert plants boast

97

an array of impressive adaptations and characteristics that enable them to survive and even thrive in the face of adversity. Ground-hugging shrubs and short sparse-leafed trees are widely separated across the desert landscape. Some of these woody plants will even shed their leaves during the hot, dry season. Annuals grow, bloom and set seed during the short season when water is available. Many perennials and bulbous plants survive heat and drought as dormant rhizomes, corms, tubers or bulbs under the ground. They will renew growing when conditions are suitable.

Many of these desert plants have either deep roots to reach underground sources of water or dense masses of wide-spreading roots near the soil surface to soak up as much moisture as possible. Cacti are especially adept at water conservation, with their broad fleshy central core for water storage; a thick waxy skin to prevent water loss; and an extensive shallow root system to capture water. Other plants, such as agaves (*Adeniums*) and euphorbias, also store water in their stems and roots, enabling them to survive long periods of drought.

The many desert regions in the world broadly include northern Africa; central and central-northwest Australia; the south and central Arabian Peninsula; the west coast region of southern Africa; northwest India and a bit to the west; east of the Caspian Sea; and other spots in northeast and north China and vicinity.

ATACAMA DESERT

Our first destination is the driest place on earth, the Atacama Desert, a virtually rainless plateau stretching in a long strip along the Pacific Ocean coast of northern Chile. Situated in the rain shadow on the leeward side of the Chilean coast range of the Andes Mountains, this desert sees an annual rainfall of less than half an inch. In some areas, no rainfall has ever been recorded. Snow and glaciers are noticeably absent and, needless to say, very little grows here, with the exception of certain species of cacti and other stalwart plants. The Atacama Desert is such a unique region that NASA has even used the area to test instruments for future missions to Mars.

The exquisite funnel-shaped blue flowers of the annual *Nolana aplocaryoides* call this region home. These lovely

Many different species of cacti live at the coast of the Atacama Desert.
GERHARD HUEDEPOHL

99

Nolana species GERHARD HUEDEPOHL

plants are adorned with small woolly green leaves to help them manage the heat. Another charming species, *Nolana elegans*, covers the landscape as far as the eye can see. This sprawling annual species also has pretty blue flowers, though these are highlighted by a white central zone.

The coastal areas of the Atacama Desert offer yet another carpet of beautiful flowers — the lovely white and pale blue blooms of the perennial *Nolana rupicola*, which fulfills most of its water needs from fog.

Nearer to the coastal mountains, the land becomes rocky and extremely dry, as it rarely sees any rainfall. The reddish-purple to pinkish flowered perennial *Cistanthe celosioides* has tiny succulent leaves that hug its sparse, sprawling stems. The flowers grow in clusters, mostly at the ends of the stems.

Not far from here, we are delighted to find several groups of a *Copiapoa* cacti. These are exquisitely highlighted

100

Cistanthe celosioides GERHARD HUEDEPOHL

by the low lighting of the late-afternoon sun, the darkened mountains, the rugged rockiness of the area and the rich blue sky above.

Copiapoa cacti species GERHARD HUEDEPOHL

101

Tillandsia landbeckii, a bromeliad GERHARD HUEDEPOHL

The sandy region of the coast has artistically undulating flats, hummocks, dunes and low-rolling hills. Randomly dispersed across this extensive landscape is a large number of highly attractive gray-blue plant spheres with narrow-leafed foliage. These plants, which consist of one species of bromeliad, *Tillandsia landbeckii*, are especially remarkable, for they survive, virtually rootless, on the sand. They derive their moisture needs exclusively from the coastal fogs that frequent the area. The mist-laden air also helps to protect these plants from the direct sun.

NAMIB DESERT

The next desert we visit is the oldest on earth, the Namib Desert. The Namib stretches along the coast of Namibia,

102

sloping toward the Atlantic Ocean. The more southerly region has many giant sand dunes, often with highly attractive red and orange sand. This coloring is caused by the concentration of iron in the sand that has oxidized over time. The older the dune, the redder the sand!

The sand is shifting all around us, and in the distance we see gravel plains and rugged mountains. As we approach the coast, some areas are enveloped in a thick fog that is a vital source of moisture for many of the desert plants here. In some years, this shroud of mist is present for more than six months.

The amazing quiver tree, *Aloe dichotoma*, native to this region, has an almost-white upper trunk and branches that appear to be coated with a powdery substance. The white color likely helps reflect some of the sun's intense heat. The lower portion of the trunk is a beautiful golden brown, peeling with many scales that are razor-sharp to protect the tree from hungry and thirsty animals.

These quiver trees have densely rounded crowns consisting of forked branches ending with sparse clusters of sharply pointed succulent green leaves. As a matter of fact, the species name *dichotoma* means *forked*. These branches and the trunk are filled with a soft permeable fiber that can store large amounts of precious water.

The especially remarkable feature of the quiver tree is

103

Aloe dichotoma, **quiver tree** DR. ROBERT T. AND MARGARET ORR © CALIFORNIA ACADEMY OF SCIENCES

its ability to conserve vital moisture during periods of extreme drought. In these conditions, the tree will actually amputate itself. It does this by first shedding the leafy ends of some of its branches, and then if drought conditions persist it will shed whole branches that would be considered expendable for the survival of the tree. Dramatic and effective!

Near the coast, where the air is often filled with a hot mistiness reminiscent of a sauna, we find scattered specimens of one of the most amazing trees on earth. At first look, it is hard to consider the wonder plant, *Welwitschia mirabilis* (syn. *W. bainesii*), a tree, for it looks more like an ugly mass of torn, tattered foliage. But a tree it is, complete with an imperceptible, short, solid-wood trunk that sometimes can be 3 feet or more in diameter. This *tree* essentially consists of two strap-like leaves, each of which has been torn into many strips and ragged shreds over many years of

104

harsh winds and other ravages of an unforgiving climate. These two leaves slowly pile up into messy heaps, and while they grow continuously from the base of the plant, they are stunted by the severity of the climate. If rolled out, each leathery ribbed leaf may be up to 8 feet long and 3 feet wide, with some specimens measuring up to 20 feet long and 6 feet wide. These huge leaves absorb considerable moisture

Welwitschia mirabilis, wonder plant DENNIS STEVENSON

from the ocean fogs that roll in. Because they are piled into large heaps, the leaves also help to keep the roots cool and therefore better able to retain moisture.

Even the roots of the wonder plant are amazing. These trees have a thick, dark-colored taproot that can reach over 6 feet deep, with many lateral roots as well. Some specimens reach 15 feet into the ground, with a few remarkable individual plants found to have taproots nearly 100 feet deep. The *Welwitschia mirabilis* is essentially a loner, growing far apart and never in colonies, which allows the lateral roots, as well as the taproot, to spread out extensively without competition for the meager water supply available in its desert home.

It is also said that this extraordinary gymnosperm can live for several thousands of years. This true survivor is found only in the Namib Desert.

AUSTRALIAN DESERTS

The largest desert region in Australia, collectively known as the Great Western Desert, includes the Great Sandy Desert, the Gibson Desert and the Great Victoria Desert. This is the world's second-largest expanse of desert, after the Sahara. Several regions of the Great Western Desert feature a characteristic red landscape of sandy dunes and plains: South Australia, the Simpson Desert in the Northern Territory and Queensland in central Australia are prime examples,

Gyrostemon ramulosus and *Grevillea stenobotrya* MEREDITH COSGROVE

as is the Gibson Desert in Western Australia.

We head over to a red-sand hills area of the Northern Territory deserts to find the shrubby *Grevillea stenobotrya*, a widespread species with cream to pale yellow flowers. Nearby we also discover *Gyrostemon ramulosus*, a shrub with yellow-green flowers. Both plants are growing on a red sand dune beneath a clear blue sky.

SOUTHWESTERN U.S. *and* NORTHERN MEXICO DESERTS

One of the deserts of North America, the Sonoran Desert, is distinguished by its forests of tall cacti. We have already visited one remarkable desert species of the region in Chapter 2. This is the birdcage plant, a species that deserves a second look for both its incredible beauty and marvelous adaptations.

We first visit a flat, fairly barren region of the Sonoran and Mojave deserts of southwestern California, Utah and

107

Geraea canescens, desert sunflower DR. AMADEJ TRNKOCZY

south into Arizona and northwestern Mexico in early spring. Here we are greeted by a dazzling display of the golden yellow flowers of the desert sunflower, *Geraea canescens*. Our timing is right for this visual treat, as the desert sunflower is an annual that will disappear once the drought and heat of summer arrives.

108

Hiking across the Mojave Desert we find a large though

Caulanthus inflatus, desert candle JOHN GAME

isolated group of the impressive desert candle, *Caulanthus inflatus*. Another annual, the desert candle is spectacular in full bloom. From a swollen yellow stem with progressively smaller leaves toward the top, grow numerous small purplish flowers.

The desert poppy, *Arctomecon merriamii*, rises from a base of hairy pale green leaves and a stout stem, each

109

Arctomecon merriamii, desert poppy
JAMES M. ANDRÉ

topped with a pristine white flower with yellow-green stamens. This pretty perennial species survives the heat and drought of summer mainly by its taproot.

Now to the Chihuahuan Desert in southern Arizona in the U.S.-Mexico border region, where two noteworthy evergreen succulents use ovoid or cylindrical stems to store water. The first of these is *Echinocereus triglochidiatus*, a low-growing, spiny, clump-forming to spreading species that shows off its green ribbed stems in full flower. And what flowers they are! Funnel- to cup-shaped, the brilliant red blooms are exquisite.

The much taller cylindrical-stemmed *Ferocactus cylindraceus*, with its warty ribs and red-orange or yellowish spines, has lovely bell-shaped flowers in shades of yellow and orange when in full bloom.

110

Echinocereus triglochidiatus JAMES M. ANDRÉ

OTHER DESERTS

The Sahara Desert is the largest in the world, stretching across northern Africa from the Atlantic coastline to the

111

Ferocactus cylindraceus JAMES M. ANDRÉ

Red Sea, while the deserts of Central Asia are unique for their frigid winters and scorching hot summers, a combination found nowhere else in the world.

Located east of the Horn of Africa, the fascinating island of Socotra and its related archipelago has an extremely dry climate, plus fierce monsoon winds carried in from Africa. Although the island has plant life not found anywhere else in the world, our focus is the species *Adenium*. The plants are practical, but pretty ugly: their contorted smooth-to-warty fat trunks and sparse leaves redeemed only by beautiful flowers. Their swollen shapes allow these repulsive yet marvelous *Adeniums* to survive long dry periods.

CHAPTER NINE

A MEDITERRANEAN PERSPECTIVE

When we imagine visiting a Mediterranean climate, many of us envision beautiful vistas of sunny seashores and rolling hills. Picturesquely gnarled olive-trees, lavender and thyme are a few of the plants that come to mind. We think of countries like Spain, Italy and Greece, especially the small, inviting villages that dot the coastline inlets. For the most part this is an accurate picture, but a Mediterranean climate is much more than olive groves and lavender fields, particularly when we consider the region from environmental, climatic and botanical perspectives.

A Mediterranean climate is most often associated with the area that surrounds the Mediterranean Sea in Europe, North Africa and parts of western Asia. Although this is correct, such a climate has come to include five distinct regions of the world, each sharing strong similarities: warm to hot dry summers, cool to mild winters with variable rain, long autumns and short springs. Even within this framework of similarities, there are still allowances for wide climatic diversity and varying seasonal conditions.

The five Mediterranean climate regions of the world are

1. The Mediterranean — often referred to as garigue or maquis;
2. Central and southern California — often referred to as chaparral;
3. Central Chile — often referred to as matorral;
4. South Africa's Cape — often referred to as fynbos;
5. Southern and southwestern Australia — often referred to as matorral or, locally, as quangong and associated with heathlands.

You'll notice that most of these regions are found between the sea or ocean and a mountain range. Those plants that grow especially close to the coast are able to tolerate the desiccating salt-laden winds that blow in from the water. Some of the adaptations here include low ground-hugging growth and small leathery or woolly leaves.

The ocean or sea also tempers climatic conditions: fog makes air humid, providing a great source of moisture for

114

plants. However, since the soil is usually rocky, gravelly or sandy, considerable moisture is lost through this sharp drainage. But airborne moisture is much better than none at all, and a coastal plant's dense hairiness or woolliness is ideal for catching the moisture in the foggy air.

Keep in mind, though, that this fog-water source applies only to plants in coastal regions. For the majority of inland Mediterranean-climate plants, adaptations to their environment require drought- and heat-tolerant strategies similar to those of the plants in deserts and other hot regions. Farther inland in Mediterranean climates, the landscape in summer can be dry and barren. Most plants here are low growing, fire adapted and drought tolerant. Other species are annuals that survive summer drought as seeds in the ground. Fire is a major ecological factor in all five Mediterranean climate regions. Some plants here protect themselves from fire by several different adaptations, such as thick, protective, low-resin bark. Other plants have become dependent on fires to stimulate growth or release seeds.

Topography and altitude also strongly affect the climatic conditions, including temperatures, that each plant experiences. For example, a plant growing in a ravine may face less wind exposure than a plant growing high up the slope of a hillside.

THE MEDITERRANEAN

The Mediterranean is composed of the whole Mediterranean basin, including a strip along the coast of northwestern Africa, and also parts of western Asia.

The Mediterranean basin area basks in warmth and sunshine during summer. If there are any clouds, they are white and fluffy, rarely bringing any rain. Because of this characteristic bright blue sky, the region has the highest solar radiation and light intensities on earth.

Through fires and the felling of trees in the region, the land degenerates into what is known as maquis or, in Italian, *macchia*. The maquis typically consists of dense thickets of low-growing or gnarled shrubs with some widely dispersed trees. The soil in this area is rocky and dry. Drought-resistant plants that prosper here include junipers, heaths, brooms, rock roses, Spanish brooms and wild olives.

Further deterioration of the maquis through erosion of even more soil results in what is known as garrigue. This is essentially a thin layer of soil over rocky ground upon which certain stalwart plants survive. Garrigue is generally found near the seashore, but it can also occur farther inland. Drought-resistant plants that thrive here include low-growing aromatic shrubby plants such as thymes, artemisias, lavenders and sages.

Cistus purpurea ROBBIN MORAN

Our first stop is southwestern Italy in June. Here, on a rocky maritime cliff, we find a large colony of the greenish-yellow flowered *Euphorbia dendroides*, tree spurge. The leaves of these rounded woody shrubs will soon dry up and fall off as a way of coping with the hot, dry summer. The plants remain in a leafless state throughout the summer, with the buds resuming growth again with the late autumn rain.

In the southeastern portion of Italy in late summer, the beautiful rock rose, *Cistus creticus*, exhibits compact low growth, which is augmented by many purple-pink, wild rose–like flowers, each with a bright yellow center. All *Cistus* species are resistant to very dry conditions.

Taking a short hike in the same vicinity, we are greeted by a group of wonderfully scented lavenders growing among the rocks. Lavenders are among the aromatic

117

Sternbergia lutea DR. AMADEJ TRNKOCZY

Mediterranean plants that secrete a water-repellent gaseous layer — essential oils — that helps to conserve water vapor on leaf surfaces.

Remaining in the same region of Italy into the autumn, the shimmering golden-yellow crocus-like flowers of *Sternbergia lutea* offer a spectacular display. Each sits atop a short stem and above grasslike leaves. This bulbous plant copes with drought by dying down during the hot, dry summer months.

CENTRAL *and* SOUTHERN CALIFORNIA

The California chaparral is a shrubland that encompasses a good portion of central and southern California, west of the Sierra Nevada mountains, and includes the northern portion of Baja California, Mexico. Some of the plants in this region include low and aromatic shrubs, such as black and white sage (*Salvia mellifera* and *S. apiana*), *Arctostaphylos* species (manzanitas) and the yellow Mariposa lily.

Traveling to the southern Sierra Nevada foothills in late spring or early summer, we are greeted by a spectacular display of yellow Mariposa lilies. The slightly bell-shaped flowers of this bulbous perennial are a rich deep yellow with maroon markings. They grow in small clusters at the ends of branching stems. We are fortunate in our timing, as soon these plants will die back, remaining underground to avoid the heat and drought of summer.

By the time we reach the southern California chaparral, it is early summer. We are pleased to come across a small grouping of the magnificent our Lord's candle, *Yucca whipplei*. This yucca species has the largest flower

Calochortus luteus, Mariposa lily NEAL KRAMER

Yucca Whipplei, our Lord's candle ROBBIN MORAN

display of any lily. Our Lord's candle is a clump-forming, monocarpic (parent plant dies after flowering), stemless plant with typical gray-green yucca foliage at the base. Its tall flower spike is especially impressive — a huge cluster of pendant, bell-shaped, fragrant, creamy white flowers.

It takes six to seven years for each *Yucca whipplei* to bloom and then the plant dies, making our visit all the more special. Even having said this, these yuccas, in any given location, are at various stages of development and plants also reproduce from offsets at the base.

CENTRAL CHILE

The central Chilean matorral is found between the moist Valdivian temperate rain forest to the south and the arid Atacama Desert to the north, with the Pacific Ocean to the west and the southern Andes Mountains to the east.

Some of the plants in this region are *Nothofagus alessandri*, *Tetilla hydrocotylifolia* and *Valdivia gayana*. The majority are endemic to central Chile's Mediterranean climate.

Our visit to Chile is to observe only one representative plant, the Chilean wine palm, *Jubaea chilensis*, in the Southern Hemisphere winter. The wine palm is native to an extremely restricted range of Chile and is threatened with extinction, which is one reason we want to see it in its natural habitat. We find a group of these special palms growing on a dry, open hillside. The Chilean wine palm has a huge dark gray trunk that is often swollen at the base and tapers toward the crown, which is dense with many blue-gray-green leaves, similar to many other palms. The large inflorescences are pendulous, consisting of separate male and female flowers.

SOUTH AFRICA'S CAPE (MOSTLY WESTERN)

South Africa's western Cape region, known as fynbos, is noted for its poor, shallow soil, yet the area boasts an extremely rich flora of incredibly beautiful plants, many of which cannot be found elsewhere. Some of the plants in this region include proteas of all sorts and colors: *Amaryllis belladonna*; *Lampranthus* species; *Bulbinella floribunda*; and the brilliantly colored monarch of the veldt, *Arctotis fastuosa*.

We now visit an open area of the fynbos to observe a

121

specimen of the national flower of South Africa, the King protea. This shrub bears many gigantic, shallow bowl–shaped, pink and snowy-white flower heads tinged with yellow. (We will visit this special plant again when we discuss fire and plants.)

SOUTHERN *and* SOUTHWESTERN AUSTRALIA

The South and Southwest Australia region, often referred to as quangong, matorral or Kwongan, is typically Mediterranean in climate, with its own unique flora. Some of the distinctive plants found here include many spectacular *Banksia* species; eucalypts of all sorts, along with Mallee scrub (multi-stemmed woody plants from ground level); the blue China orchid, *Caladenia gemmata*; and the many-flowered fringe lily, *Thysanotus multiflorus*.

Our travels in the Australian Mediterranean climate focus on finding a few of the spectacular species of *Banksia*. First, let us familiarize ourselves with some of the common attributes that most species share: they are mostly evergreen shrubs or small trees with leathery leaves; their flowers grow in dense clusters surrounding cylindrical flower spikes; and their fruits are large woody cones that can be highly impressive.

The first species we come across, growing on a rocky slope in the Stirling Range, is *B. solandri*, with its oak-like

leaves and large, striking bronze-colored flower clusters. Next, we are fortunate to find a small group of the large shrub species *B. brownii*, with fern-like leaves and dense red to reddish-brown flower spikes. Moving on to the vicinity surrounding Albany in Western Australia, we are privileged to encounter three wonderful specimens of the threatened *Banksia verticillata* growing beside granite outcroppings.

Banksia coccinia in New South Wales, Australia DENNIS STEVENSON

These are large shrubs with multiple branches surrounded by whorls of leathery leaves. The plant's golden flower spikes are gorgeous. This *Banksia* species perishes quickly in humid conditions or where there is poor soil drainage, which indicates that it is a true heat- and drought-tolerant plant suited to a Mediterranean climate.

We now know that Mediterranean climates encompass much more than picturesque vistas. Mediterranean climates are found around the world, from California to Chile, and from South Africa's Cape to Australia. Each of these regions offers its own plant diversity, adaptations, wonder and appeal.

CHAPTER TEN

AN ENDURING CHAMPION

Imagine standing high up on the side of a mountain, where strong winds blow ceaselessly all around you, regardless of the season, and thunder and lightning storms are frequent. Winters are bitterly cold, to $-15°F$, and summers are extremely dry, with daytime highs of about $55°F$. Precipitation is a mere 10 inches a year, mostly in the form of winter snow. The trees all around you are gnarled and ragged from enduring ages of unforgiving, relentless environmental extremes. Such is the home of the bristlecone pine, *Pinus longaeva*, particularly those trees found here in the White Mountain range of southeastern California and southwestern Nevada.

Bristlecone pines here grow right at the edge of the final timberline at 7,500 to 11,900 feet, not far from the summit

125

Pinus longaeva, bristlecone pine DR. AMADEJ TRNKOCZY

of the mountains. In the rain shadow of the Sierra Nevada, trees are exposed to nearly persistent drought. On any given day in the summer, the amount of moisture in the air is about half a millimeter — the barest fraction of an inch. This is the lowest air moisture content ever recorded anywhere. As if that were not enough, the soil on which these trees stand is rocky and barren, making it difficult to grab

126

a foothold. Where there is soil, the roots mostly manage to descend only 2 to 7 inches below the surface, spreading in all directions to find whatever moisture is available. The White Mountain range California bristlecone pines are among the hardiest and toughest trees on earth. True enduring champions that survive the harsh environment of an alpine desert.

Pinus longaeva is also found in other areas of southeast California, southern Nevada and Utah. A close cousin, the Rocky Mountain bristlecone pine, *P. aristata*, grows at elevations from 7,000 to 12,000 feet above sea level in Arizona, Nevada and New Mexico. A synonym for *P. longaeva* is *P. aristata* var. *longaeva*, which shows just how intimately related the two species are. Differences are minor; *P. aristata* has shorter needles that are usually covered with white dots of dried resin, more so than those of *P. longaeva*.

Living a long life even in the face of adversity is a survival strategy of the bristlecone pine. Returning to the White Mountains in southern California, we find a handful of these stalwart trees that are estimated to be around 5,000 years old — this would make certain specimens older than the Egyptian pyramids. One especially venerable tree is appropriately known as Methuselah, named for a Biblical figure who lived 969 years. Methuselah the tree is the oldest living bristlecone pine — 4,800 years old and still going

127

strong. The bristlecone pine is considered by many to be the oldest living thing on Earth.

The age of these remarkable trees was determined by the accurate method of counting annual tree rings. Next time you purchase a cut Christmas tree, just look at the base of the trunk and count the rings of growth. This will determine how old the tree was before it was cut down. Most often Christmas trees are cut down in the prime of their lives, five to eight years of age.

Early in the 19th century, scientists first observed that differing widths of growth rings were directly related to conditions experienced by the tree during each year of its growth. Dendrochronology, the study of tree rings to determine past climatic events and their approximate dates, was thus born. Each year a tree adds one ring of wood to its trunk, producing the annual rings seen in a cross-section of the trunk. The tree rings on a bristlecone pine are exceedingly numerous and thin. Often a microscope is required to count them. This narrow spacing between tree rings demonstrates the severity of the climatic conditions the tree endured over thousands of years. The highest ring count reported was 4,844 years from a felled tree in the Humboldt National Forest of eastern Nevada. Later studies indicated that this tree must have been at least 5,100 years old.

To count the annual rings on living trees, scientists

have developed a thin metal rod, known as a borer. This yard-long, pencil-thin instrument takes a series of radial cores from a tree, allowing dendrochronologists not only to determine the tree's age, but also to get a glimpse of past climatic events that may have occurred in the region where the tree grows. By using this method — which does no damage to the tree — scientists have determined that several bristlecone pines are 4,000 to 5,000 years old, particularly those in California's White Mountains.

The bristlecone pine's growth rate is incredibly slow, with about 1,100 annual growth rings in the space of 5 inches. A 16-year-old plant may be only 4 feet high and may attain a scant inch in diameter after a century of growth. Bristlecone pines are usually short, about 18 feet tall, though some specimens grow up to over 30 feet, with a girth of about 4 feet. A few unique individuals are even taller and broader.

The gnarled trunks and limbs of bristlecone pines are so strong that they almost never break. Even their needles are uncommonly tough, persisting on the tree for ten to 30 years or longer before falling off. These old needles can still photosynthesize.

Diseases and pests are virtually unknown to the bristlecone pine, largely because of the tree's dense, highly resinous wood. Lightning strikes and fire are also of little concern to the bristlecone pine's survival. Because the trees are so widely spaced, any fire caused by a lightning strike is restricted to only one tree. Also, nothing else is able to grow at the base of the trees, and fallen needles are few, so there is little litter on the ground to spread a fire to other trees.

An individual bristlecone pine continues to survive its harsh climate in a seemingly determined manner, even though a considerable portion of its main trunk will have been dead for up to several thousand years. Often, a single branch, attached to the original tree's roots, takes over the tree's life processes to ensure survival and continuance.

CHAPTER ELEVEN
A FIRM FOOTING

When we think of plants having a firm footing, roots come to mind first, though the term can also apply to several other plant adaptations that demonstrate a species' determination to grab on and survive in the face of adversity or environmental challenges.

Our first trip is a bit different than any of the others we have taken, for we are heading to the City Hall property in downtown Toronto, Canada. We are immediately struck by the vast expanse of gray concrete that lies before us, with the space-age "flying saucer" centerpiece and the hangar-like design of the buildings in the background. Walking toward these structures, we are surprised to find a single tiny flowering dandelion that has somehow forced its way through the thick concrete. Such colossal strength

131

from a tiny plant seems impossible, yet we see this phenomenon frequently. Most of us have witnessed this incredible demonstration of strength in our driveways, on sidewalks or at vacant building sites. Also think of the many open squares or plazas around the world with expanses of concrete or brick. Watch any abandoned or neglected site and, over time, green plant life will establish itself, often covering previously unsightly objects with their beauty.

ROCK SPLITTERS

The young roots of many rock-splitter plants are amazing in that they creep, tightly pressed against sheer rock surfaces, and then squeeze into virtually imperceptible cracks and crevices until even huge boulders and mountain slopes are split apart. Other rock splitters grow in rocky outcroppings and are able to split the boulders and rocks into smaller and smaller pieces in their determination to get a secure footing in their rugged environment. Over time, some of the rock-splitting trees and shrubs have actually helped to shape the landscape around the world.

The most noteworthy rock splitters are in the *Eucalyptus* and *Ficus* genera. Let us take a trip to Australia to observe a few of these plants in their natural habitat. Our first destination is the south coast region of Western Australia. Here we find the shrubby Twin Peak Island Mallee, *Eucalyptus*

132

insularis, growing on some rock domes in very shallow soil, in rock crevices and at the base of rocky cliffs. We next head to the north coast, where we encounter the tropical red box, *Eucalyptus brachyandra*. The group of small scraggly trees we come upon are growing on an extremely unfavorable site at the tops of some rocky ridges and the edges of sandstone escarpments. Next, we will remain on the coast,

only now a little inland from New South Wales. Here we find a group of scribbly gum, *Eucalyptus haemastoma*. These small trees are growing in the very shallow soils of a steep slope, into whose deep fissures the tree roots can penetrate. This species is noted for its capacity to exist on the rockiest sites.

We have plenty of time, so let's travel to further regions of Oceania to discover even more rock splitters. Our first stop is an exposed area of central northern Australia, where summers are hot and dry, and

Ficus platypoda, rock fig MEREDITH COSGROVE

Corymbia aparrerinja,
ghost gum MEREDITH COSGROVE

winters are cold. Here we find a single small tree of the rock fig, *Ficus platypoda*, bravely holding on to an almost vertical rock cliff, its grayish roots trailing and clinging for support. Traveling south into central Australia we find several ghost gums, *Corymbia aparrerinja*, also clinging precariously to a sheer rock face. These small scraggly trees have a smooth powdery white or cream-colored bark that sheds in thin patches.

Although Alpine snow gum, *Eucalyptus pauciflora*, is rarely referred to as a rock splitter, we must head over to southeastern Australia to see this highly attractive plant in its native habitat. The specimen we come across, with its twisted branches and broad trunk, is growing well among the rocks. What we find particularly special about this species is the wonderfully attractive bark that comes in a wide range of colors on different trees. The smooth bark may be reddish brown to whitish gray, peeling

134

Eucalyptus pauciflora, Alpine snow gum MEREDITH COSGROVE

in irregular patches and strips to reveal white, beige, bronze, yellow or greenish underbark.

From there we go to central southeast Africa, where we discover a rock-splitter fig representative, the large-leaved rock fig, *Ficus abutilifolia*. Growing among rocks and boulders, this small contorted tree has whitish powdery to flaky bark. Not far from here is a modest group of the hairy rock fig, *Ficus glumosa*. These shrubs and small trees with smooth pale gray or cream-colored trunks appear to be growing happily on a rocky outcropping. Over to a rocky — or perhaps boulder-like — hillside in eastern Namibia, where we discover a single specimen of *Sterculia quinqueloba*. This small tree is impressive in its ability to establish a footing on such rugged terrain. The tree's bark is flaky and a lovely smooth white to cream color. After a long, hot trek west across the Namib Desert, we come across several of the rock-splitting figs,

135

Ficus abutifolia, large-leaved rock fig WILLEM FROST

Ficus ilicina. True rock splitters, these creeping shrubs hug the ground and are found only on rocks. This group is growing on a rock slope as well as in nearby rocky outcrops.

Often there are trees and plants that, although not labeled as rock splitters, still demonstrate an amazing ability to grow in rocky areas and even on sheer rock cliffs or the slopes of mountains. Such habitats would pose a severe challenge to the survival of most other plants.

ANCHORING

One of the many functions of roots is to anchor the plant to the ground in which it grows. But there are also other ways that plants get a firm footing, as we will see. Let us go on journeys of discovery to observe several of these unique anchoring plants around the world.

Our first destination is a moist, sandy beach on the

136

Sterculia quinqueloba MEREDITH COSGROVE

western coast of one of the Queen Charlotte Islands, British Columbia, to observe the fascinating yellow sand verbena, *Abronia latifolia*, in its native habitat. We are delighted to see a large number of these mat-forming, trailing plants, all in full bloom, with their rubbery stems spreading in all directions across the sand within a few yards above the high-tide mark. The exquisite flowers are in dense rounded clusters of bright yellow to slightly orange. But it is their fragrance that really captures our attention. As we stoop closer, their aroma is enticingly sweet and not to be forgotten, blending wonderfully with the scent of the salty sea air. The leaves are thick and fleshy, oval to kidney-shaped, opposite along the stems. The yellow sand verbena has a thick, deep taproot that helps prevent the plants from being washed away. Both the leaves and stems are covered with sticky glandular hairs that further anchor the plants to their

137

Abronia latifolia, yellow sand verbena NEAL KRAMER

windy, insecure sandy abode. These sticky hairs help plants hold on to grains of sand that can weigh as much as the plant itself.

Lingering a bit longer on the Queen Charlotte Islands, and after a hike along the beaches here, we are lucky enough to discover a small grouping of the highly unusual beach silvertop, *Glehnia leiocarpa*. Before we take a closer look at this plant, it is worth recognizing that the beach silvertop has many specialized adaptations to an often harsh environment that includes salt spray, shifting sands and extreme desiccation. Unseen beneath the sands, this plant has an extensive deep root system, including a stout woody taproot that stores reserves of water. Now looking at these prostrate spreading plants, we see that each has

Glehnia leiocarpa, beach silvertop NICKOLAY KURZENKO

QUIVER
TREES

a short, almost nonexistent stem. The thick leathery and waxy basal leaves are densely woolly beneath, lobed and coarsely toothed. Several sheathing leaf stalks are buried below, serving as anchors in the shifting sands. Each of these adaptations helps the plants in reducing water loss. The hairy-stalked small white flowers grow in several compact clusters.

After a short hike, we come across a grouping of the exquisite hairy cinquefoil, *Potentilla villosa*, growing exposed at the summit of a rocky cliff, with salt-laden sea air blowing around us. This species, common throughout much of northwest North America, is noted for its ability to cling to the slightest cracks in solid rock. The common name is definitely fitting, for these mounding perennials are virtually covered with long, soft silvery hairs that help reduce transpiration and moisture loss. This woolly coat also helps these plants to resist the effects of salt spray in coastal areas. The smallish-lobed, tooth-edged and hairy leaves mostly grow densely together. The flowers are a brilliant hue of golden yellow with a spot of glowing orange at the base of each and appear in clusters above the highly attractive foliage. Seeing the hairy cinquefoil in its native habitat has been a real treat.

We now fly over to some coastal bluffs in Ireland to observe an exceptionally interesting annual, the burrowing clover, *Trifolium subterranean*. This delightful prostrate to

140

Potentilla villosa, hairy cinquefoil JIM RILEY

creeping plant has shamrock or three-lobed cloverleaves. Both the leaves and stems are covered in silvery white hairs, while the flowers are pure white to creamy pink–tinged, pea-like and in clusters of two or three florets. Though the burrowing clover has a taproot, it has another effective way to anchor itself to the sandy or gravelly soil in which it usually grows. The flowering stems bend over until the flowers

Trifolium subterranean,
burrowing clover STEVE MATSON

form a sharp kink with the stem, while still facing upward. When the flowers wither, scale-like bracts develop and grow downward and outward into the soil like the flukes of an anchor. This effectively holds the plant to the ground and also pulls the developing fruit into the soil in the process. As a result, the plant sows its own seeds. So, as you can see, the plant's common name and specific name are apt.

Most of us know the delicious-tasting fruits of the blackberry plant, *Rubus fruticosus*, but few of us are aware of its aggressive tendencies in establishing a firm footing in its native environment. To observe wild blackberries, let us visit the border between the U.S. and Canada in southwestern British Columbia and northwestern Washington State. The entire length of the property along the border here is overgrown with a natural 8- to 10-foot-high and deep barrier hedge of blackberry plants. Crossing the border here

142

would prove to be folly, for the dense tangle of scrambling thorny branches would most certainly tear both clothing and skin. Blackberry plants can grow exceedingly fast, about 2 inches per day. The stems have sharp backward-pointing spines that grasp onto nearby vegetation, rocks and virtually anything else in their path. The plants often overwhelm other species by clambering over and hooking onto them. And when the stems come into contact with the ground, small rootlets develop at the nodes, creating many new plants. These aggressive tendencies are best demonstrated through the slow motion of time-lapse photography: the blackberry plant appears to sense the presence of other plants and objects and reaches out with its branches and stems to wrap around or smother them.

The depth of a plant's root system may give a good indication of just how firm a footing the plant has in the ground. Here are a couple of examples of deep root systems that far exceed the systems of the vast majority of trees and other plants. During the building of the Suez Canal in Central America, an unspecified species of tamarisk was recorded as having roots that extended to the phenomenal depth of 164 feet. Another story has it that during construction work in South Africa, many years ago now, a gigantic unnamed species of fig was found to have had the longest taproot ever seen, growing straight down into the earth for some

Populus tremuloides, quaking aspen LOUIS-M. LANDRY

400 feet. If this is true, it is most probable that the taproot had to force its way through rock at some point.

Perhaps the epitome of a plant anchoring to the ground is the quaking aspen, *Populus tremuloides*. To observe these fast-growing trees, we head to a 106-acre quaking aspen grove near Salt Lake City, Utah. This tree spreads extensively by suckers or runners — it has about 47,000 stems

144

that sprout from the roots of one original tree. Therefore all of these trees are linked, as if by thousands of inter-connecting umbilical cords. Many consider this grove of trees as a single living organism. If so, this quaking aspen grove is the largest living organism on Earth. Or is each tree growing independently? It all depends on your perspective.

STRANGLERS

Can you imagine a tree, vine or other plant strangling another tree? Well, as we will soon see, such activity happens in many regions of the world. Let us examine a selection of these stranglers.

Most notorious of the often amazing fig species are those known as stranglers. Many of these can be beautiful, especially if their seed germinates on open land where they grow as normal, attractive trees. However, their bad reputation is deserved. Most strangler species begin life as epiphytes, in the canopy of the forest. Their seed is usually dispersed high above the forest floor through bird or bat droppings or carried there inadvertently by monkeys and other animals. The strangler's seed germinates in the canopy of other trees, after settling into a crook or crack in the host tree's branches or upper trunk. These seedlings develop long aerial roots that cling and wrap around the host tree. They continue growing rapidly downward in this fashion until they finally reach the ground

145

Ficus watkinsiana as strangler

and soil far below, at which point these aerial roots become true roots. Then former aerial roots become stems, which thicken and strengthen their grip around the host tree, forming an interlacing network of branches. This effectively prevents the host tree from growing and essentially crushes it to death. Some have likened this type of fig to a vegetable boa constrictor. This description is quite apt! Eventually, the now-dead host tree rots away, and what remains is remarkable to observe, as now only the fig tree is left standing. This is a towering, latticed network of the strangler fig's branches, encircling a hollow core where the host tree once stood.

We find the gray fig, *Ficus virens*, on the Solomon Islands and more in northern Australia. Each tree we observe has heavy limbs and drooping branches. One of the most famous specimens is the curtain fig tree of the Atherton tableland near the Cairns tourist area in Queensland. The wild plants of the gray fig, like several other species of strangler fig, often start off as epiphytes, high in the forest canopy. They grow on the host tree, but do not receive their nourishment from it. In rare instances, these epiphytic plants are in too difficult a position and are unable to begin

Ficus virens as a banyan M. FAGG © AUSTRALIAN NATIONAL BOTANIC GARDENS

wrapping their roots around the host tree. In these cases, they may quickly send a single root straight down like a long rope. Once it reaches the ground and becomes firmly rooted, it sends out side shoots toward the host tree's trunk and begins the strangling process. It appears as though the strangler senses the host tree's presence. A long struggle ensues, though the strangler fig eventually overpowers the host tree by sheer strength. The vegetable boa constrictor strikes again!

Further strangler figs include the weeping or Benjamin's fig, *Ficus benjamina*, of tropical Asia, which is also a popular indoor houseplant, and *Ficus watkinsiana*, found mostly along the coast in the rain forests of northeast Queensland and northeast New South Wales. Many of these strangler fig species also feature a wide-spreading root system underground, which can only add to the chagrin of their host trees. These stranglers seem to have a nearly insatiable want for nutrients and moisture.

Traveling to the north island of New Zealand, we find the rata vine, *Metrosideros robusta*, which can eventually grow into a tree. As we arrive in summer, the tree is adorned with masses of beautiful orange-red flowers. The rata vine begins life as an epiphyte from a bird-deposited seed in the bark of a host tree, high in the forest canopy. The aerial roots clamber down and around the host tree's trunk to reach the ground and become true roots at the tree's base. After several years, the former aerial roots expand, merging to form a huge trunk. The host tree is squeezed to death. The rata is now a large tree on its own, as we see before us, where once there was a host tree that has since rotted away.

Found throughout much of the tropical regions of the world, particularly rain-forest areas, *Mucuna* species are mostly woody climbing vines known as lianas. These bat-pollinated flowering lianas also begin life as epiphytes before becoming stranglers. The often beautiful flower clusters and resultant pods hang down from their hosts on long rope-like stems. Their seeds drift across the oceans to wash ashore on distant beaches and islands. Just a sampling of *Mucuna* stranglers include *M. urens*, *M. sloanei* and *M. pruriens*. Depending on the species, flower color can range from red, purple, white and more. *M. giganteum* is a creamy-white-flowered species found in Maui, Hawaii, mostly in rain-forest areas. *M. bennettii* in Papau, New Guinea, provides a dazzling display of orangey-red pea-like flower clusters.

A very different type of strangler is found in many forested areas of western North America. After a short hike in the forests of western Oregon, we come across a group of trees with several orange honeysuckle vines, *Lonicera ciliosa*, clambering up them. These are really quite pretty, with dense clusters of trumpet-shaped orange flowers. They are

149

Lonicera ciliosa, orange honeysuckle vine clambering on host BEN LEGLER

not like the other stranglers we have visited, for these start life in the soil below. But as they climb up the trees, the orange honeysuckle wraps tightly around each tree's trunk. These vines can easily strangle the very tree upon which they climb for support. The tight coiling around a tree's trunk often interferes with or even prevents the flow, through photosynthesis and related processes, of nutrient material from the green leaves above the twining portion of the vine. Below the orange honeysuckle's coiling stems, the trees are deprived of the nutrients normally supplied by the leaves and as a result the tree under the strangling branches will eventually dry up and die.

BANYANS

Imagine a tree with a canopy so massive that under its shade an entire village can find shelter. Our visit to India brings us

150

to a magnificent fig tree known as the Indian banyan, *Ficus benghalensis*, that fits this description. Observe that as the more horizontal branches of the Indian banyan extend, fine vertical aerial roots develop at intervals along their length. These grow down until they touch the ground, where they develop true roots. Once established, these rapidly develop into secondary trunks to the main tree. Notice the

Ficus benghalensis, Indian banyan tree, at The Valley School, Bangalore DELONIX/CC-BY-SA 3.0

similarity to the growth process of the strangler figs we just discussed. These pillar-like secondary trunks are required to support the original tree's enormous canopy, which can cover several acres. The tree continues to spread outward in this fashion, seemingly indefinitely. This old tree is about 70 feet high, which only adds to its impressive stature. In the Andhra Valley in India, one tree is recorded as having a crown that measured 2,000 feet in circumference, supported by 320 secondary trunks.

In addition to the large pillar-like secondary trunks, a typical Indian banyan, such as our specimen, may also have about 3,000 or more slender aerial roots dangling like curtains from its branches. The Indian banyans are also distinguished by their venerable life span, which may reach 300 to 400 years.

The term *banyan* does not refer only to the Indian banyan tree — it also identifies a manner of growth. There are several other trees, almost exclusively figs, that also exhibit aerial roots and trunks from the branches as extra support for the often immense spreading canopy. The Indian banyan rightfully is the most famous and also the most common. A few of the other *Ficus* species that may also develop the aerial root habit that is synonymous with the term *banyan* include the Chinese banyan or Indian laurel tree, *F. microcarpa*; the Bo fig, peepul or sacred fig, *F. religiosa*; the Gray

152

fig, *F. virens*, which is more often a strangler; and even the Indian Rubber tree or rubber plant, *F. elastica*.

BUTTRESSES *and* SNAKY ROOTS

Buttresses are extensions of the main trunk of a tree that extend outward to provide extra support. They often continue outward to form what are referred to as snaky roots, which also provide support for the massive size many of these trees can attain. These lateral surface roots predominate and can extend as far as 200 feet from the main trunk. A taproot usually develops in a tree's seedling stage, but this gradually rots away in the damp soil.

Many trees, particularly in rain-forest regions, have huge buttressed trunks and snaky roots to help support them in the frequently shallow soils of their habitat. Figs are especially noted for these traits. Our travels to see one of these fig trees take us to the coastal rain forests of Eastern Australia, where we find the Moreton Bay fig or Australian banyan, *Ficus macrophylla*. This huge spreading evergreen species has both a buttressed trunk and extensive roots. Its snaky roots are thick, slithering and curving along the ground for a considerable distance. This adaptation is most likely a result of the soil being too difficult for easy root penetration and anchorage, making support for the

153

Ficus aurea, strangler fig buttresses at Rincon de la Vieja, Costa Rica HANS HILLEWAERT / CC-BY-SA-3.0

great size of the tree mandatory. The Moreton Bay fig can also be a strangler or a banyan.

Just a couple of other trees that often exhibit huge buttresses and snaky roots include the golden fig, *Ficus aurea*, frequently a strangler in its native West Indies and Florida, and the spiny-trunked kapok or silk-cotton tree, *Ceiba pentadra*, originally of Africa.

ON STILTS

Let's head to the mangrove swamps of Florida to observe *Rhizophora mangle*. Upon arrival we are confronted by a forest of both tall and short mangle trees, with their densely tangled prop roots intertwined above the water level. We will leave our boat at the edge of this flooded forest, for

155

Rhizophora mangle, mangrove ROBBIN MORAN

even hiking by foot will prove difficult. The many aerial prop roots of these mangle trees provide much-needed support for the trees in their shallow watery to mucky soil environment. Such forest floods may be seasonal or year-round and are often a result of overflowing lakes, streams and other waterways in lowland regions.

Finally, we visit flooded lowland regions of the Seychelles and Madagascar to see another plant on stilts, *Pandanus utilis*, in its native habitat. These plants also have thick aerial prop roots for support, as well as attractive spirally arranged palm-like leaves. Many other *Pandanus* species have stilt roots exposed well above the water level, including *P. tectorius* in the Eastern Australia coastal regions.

Pandanus utilis DENNIS STEVENSON

As we have observed, plants are remarkable in their ability to establish a firm footing in their often difficult and challenging habitats.

CHAPTER TWELVE

CHEMISTRY

Chemistry is intimately involved with everything in existence. From the far reaches of the cosmos to individual stars (including our sun), to the depths of the oceans, to all living creatures and non-living matter on earth, to the most minute atom, chemistry plays a part. Far too complex a subject for us to discuss at any length here! Even so, it is fascinating how plants either use or manufacture different chemicals and compounds to grow, adapt, survive and thrive in their environment.

About 70,000 different kinds of chemicals have been identified in plants, and no doubt many more exist. Within the plants themselves, a myriad of chemical processes take place, virtually each and every day of their growing lives. Just a few of these include the wonder of photosynthesis, protein synthesis and nutrient absorption. Then there are the chemical exchanges between water, air and soil, and, finally, the exchange of nutrients.

Many plants manufacture their own chemicals and compounds to survive their environment. The antifreeze-like liquid produced by many plants to help them endure the bitter cold of winter comes to mind here. Many more plants develop deliciously fragrant flowers or nectar rich in sugars in order to attract pollinators. Several other plants produce chemicals to repel or even kill insect or animal threats to their survival. Still others develop a unique resistance or tolerance to certain chemicals and conditions that would prove toxic to most other species.

PHOTOSYNTHESIS *and* CHLOROPHYLL

Of all the chemical processes of plants, photosynthesis is the most wondrous — ultimately all life on earth is dependent upon it. Let us reflect for a moment on the important roles of air and water in this vital-to-life process of photosynthesis. Basically, photosynthesis involves plants using carbon dioxide plus water to react with light energy from the sun and plant chloroplasts (containing chlorophyll) to make plant growth possible. Carbohydrates, starches, sugars and other organic compounds or foods for the plant's growth are all a result of the chemical processes of

158

photosynthesis. Through this process, plants also release oxygen, which replenishes our atmosphere with this essential element that is absolutely vital to all life.

Chlorophyll is intimately involved in photosynthesis. As children, many of us asked why plants are green. The answer is really quite simple — plant leaves contain a green substance known as chlorophyll, a word which essentially means *green of the leaf*. White light is partly made up of the complementary colors red and green; chlorophyll absorbs considerable amounts of the former and reflects the latter. This is why we see plants as the beautiful and soothing color green. Different types, intensities or combinations of chlorophyll and other chemicals determine whether a plant appears yellow, green, blue-green or rich green. The plant's chlorophyll uses red light because it is the form of energy plants need to turn carbon dioxide and water into foods like sugars and starches. When you purchase fluorescent plant grow-lights, you will notice that they most often lean to the red end of the spectrum. Keep in mind, though, that plants also use other colors of light from the light spectrum, plus other chemicals for their growth processes.

HORMONES

We humans sometimes tend to blame our moods and actions on hormones. This is not the case with plants, or

159

at least we hope not. But who knows, maybe plants can be moody too. Plants manufacture chemical hormones for a great variety of purposes. For example, along with RNA, hormones help to regulate protein synthesis and other functions within the plant. There are even wound hormones that rapidly heal injuries a plant may sustain.

The main growth hormone manufactured by plants is auxin, from the Greek *auxein*, which means to grow. This water-soluble chemical is transported to the growing tips and roots of plants. It encourages stems to grow up and roots to grow down. If one were to remove the growing tips of a plant, upward growth would cease and lateral branches would grow more quickly. This response can be observed when we pinch or prune the tips of plants to increase branching and encourage a more full plant. Auxin is also involved in promoting fruit formation and the maturation of the embryo in a seed. Again, auxin is only one of many chemical processes involved in plant growth.

Some plants have the amazing ability to defend themselves from insect attacks by manufacturing their own specialized hormones that serve as an effective insect control or repellent. Here we cover just two examples. The first is the fragrant balsam fir, *Abies balsamea*, of eastern to central North American forests. This tree secretes a hormone that prevents insect larvae from maturing and, therefore, from

160

reproducing. The other is a popular bedding plant annual, *Ageratum*. This pretty plant manufactures a hormone that speeds an insect's larvae development to an adult state, which renders it dwarfed and sterile in the process. They can't do much damage in that condition.

Ageratum houstonianum, *floss flower* NICKOLAY KURZENKO

Another fascinating aspect of plant hormones is their intricate involvement in winter hardiness, particularly for deciduous plants. Autumn is when many of these trees and other plants drop their leaves, preparing for the frigid winter months. If the plants do not lose their leaves, ice crystals can puncture cell membranes and kill plant cells. The process of losing leaves and then setting a protective seal over the scars where the leaf was once held is known as leaf abscission. As temperatures lower and day length shortens in autumn, hormones that regulate the abscission process are stimulated into production. The protective seal prevents

161

loss of water from the plant stems and hinders entry by harmful fungi and insect larvae. During abscission, plants also produce chemicals that have essentially the same effect as the antifreeze we use in our cars. This plant antifreeze consists of a concentrated sugar solution that prevents the water in plants from freezing.

In spring, other hormones reverse this process — the plant antifreeze is replaced by a solution that consists mainly of water for the warmer seasons, the protective seal is shed and buds develop. With the chemical manufacturing processes in full swing, the plant's growth resumes. This considerable activity is stimulated by the higher temperatures and longer days that spring brings.

AUTUMN COLORS

Keeping our focus on deciduous leaves, let's discuss the chemical processes involved in providing us with such a vivid display of color in the autumn. Once again, cooler temperatures and shorter days stimulate the chemical processes that produce these brilliant color changes we so greatly appreciate. The process begins when the normal green pigment in leaves, chlorophyll, begins to decompose, revealing orange, red and yellow pigments. These were also present in the leaves during spring and summer but were hidden by the more abundant chlorophyll. The different-colored leaves on the various

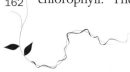

species of plants are affected mainly by the varying amounts of red, orange or yellow present in them. In some trees, brilliant red pigments are produced either with the orange and yellow or separately. Carotenoid pigments give the golden color to certain trees and plants, while anthocyanin pigments predominate in red-leaved trees because they hide the carotenoid pigments. The process is wonderful to observe, as we thoroughly enjoy these vivid autumn colors.

ALKALOIDS

Another group of chemicals that plants manufacture are alkaloids. Several of these have proven medicinal benefits, even though they are most often toxic or poisonous. There are thousands of alkaloids, and probably many more that have not yet been discovered. They are common in plants, though their function is still not fully understood. Several scientists believe they may help to protect plants from parasites and predators — this would stand to reason, considering some of the toxic alkaloids with which we are familiar. It's a classic example of plants developing chemicals for their own protection.

We will cover only one alkaloid here, colchicine. This alkaloid is derived from the pretty blue- to purplish-flowered autumn crocus bulb, *Colchicum autumnale*, and is used in plant breeding to alter gene structure. Colchicine was the

163

Colchium autumnale, autumn crocus

first mutation maker, and it can increase a plant's chromosome number. Because the poisonous colchicine compound affects the division of cell nuclei, it is used in the treatment of certain forms of cancer.

Although the flowers of the autumn crocus are similar in appearance to those of the common crocus, the two plants are not related. One blooms in the early spring, the other in autumn. The common crocus, *Crocus sativus*, is the source of the expensive spice saffron.

RESISTANCE *and* TOLERANCE

A few remarkable plants have the extraordinary ability to either resist or tolerate the toxic effects of certain poisons or metals, or an excess of specific minerals or elements in the soil. Some plants even actually absorb certain poisonous substances with little to no ill effect. Any other plants simply

164

could not grow and would surely succumb under these conditions. Yet these stalwart plants survive and even thrive.

JOURNEYS *of* DISCOVERY

Our first visit will be to northern British Columbia. The rolling hills and meadows before us are covered with brilliantly colored lupine flower spikes in a dazzling array of blue, purple, pink and white. The sun behind us and the dark clouds above serve only to intensify the exquisite beauty of this scene. To augment our enjoyment even further, rugged mountain peaks in the distance and dense stretches of deep green coniferous forest off to the sides add bold contrast.

Our purpose in making this trip is to better appreciate the beauty of the lupines in their natural environment, before addressing their amazing ability to absorb toxic substances from the soil. After the Chernobyl nuclear disaster in Ukraine in 1986, Russian scientists planted several unnamed species of lupine around the site, for the sole purpose of absorbing radiation poison from the soil. After the lupines had successfully achieved their purpose, the plants were then dug up, root and all, and buried far from any populated location. If lupines can help to clean these toxic soils, they can certainly improve some of our contaminated soils as well. The plant's incredible ability can also be used to absorb excess pesticides and other toxic poisons from the soil.

165

We now head south to an arid riparian region of southern California. The spring weather is a bit hot and dry as we approach a row of large shrubby *Tamarix parviflora*, growing on rocky, sandy terrain near a slow-moving stream. Their gracefully arching branches are smothered in tiny, soft, fluffy-looking pink flower spikes. This is but one of several tamarisk species introduced from Europe; some have become naturalized to the point of invasiveness. The remarkable tamarisks are capable of thriving in places where the water table contains over 20 percent salts. They will grow in saline soils, such as we find here, that would be toxic to most other plants.

One reason tamarisks are able to thrive in soil with a high salt content is because they possess something similar to glands, through which surplus salt is excreted. As a matter of fact, soil can be biologically desalinated by growing salt-absorbing plants like tamarisk and seablite and then harvesting them. Most tamarisk species are also tolerant of hot, dry and windy seashore conditions, mainly because of their deep taproots.

Traveling closer to the coast, still in spring, we find the sea plantain, *Plantago maritima*, growing on the fringes of saltwater flats. This is another plant with the amazing ability to absorb excess salts. Also introduced from Europe, sea plantain can survive saltwater flooding and lengthy submergence in brackish or fresh water. The widely spaced

166

Tamarix parviflora, tamarix JOHN GAME

plants that we have found growing on the sandy coastal soil each consists of a dense rosette of grasslike foliage, with compact greenish-yellow flower spikes. The sea plantain has a deep taproot that helps the plant to anchor to the soil.

Let us now turn our attention to some plants that have the unique ability to tolerate or resist the toxic effects of certain metallic elements in their environment. We find

167

several of the low-growing sandwort or vernal, *Minuartia verna*, happily growing on the debris at an abandoned lead workings in southern England. *Minuartia verna* is a pretty little plant with an abundance of small white flowers in early spring and grasslike foliage. This species of sandwort is fully resistant to the toxic levels of copper found in the soil at sites such as this. No other type of plant could tolerate it. This is why, in soils containing an excess of copper, no other plants are found in the vicinity.

There are two plants that are actually gluttons for the heavy metal–element nickel. Each can absorb up to 10 percent of its dry weight, with no observable ill effects. To see one of these, we first head to southern Spain in late spring where we find the perennial madwort, *Alyssum bertolonii*, growing in a rocky area. The group of plants we discover are practically smothered with heads of tiny white and cream flowers. Next we visit New Zealand, where the shrub violet, *Hybanthus floribundus*, is found, again in a rocky area. The plants have exquisite light blue and pale lilac orchid-like flowers, which are used extensively in the Oceania region's cut-flower trade.

Another heavy metal–element that is not required by plants (though unfortunately readily accumulated by them) and is particularly associated with alkaline soils is selenium. Chemical studies have shown that soils drained from certain shales contain concentrations of this element. Toxic

168

levels are indicated by white leaves on plants and the death of rodents that have fed on the plants. Amazingly, there are several species of milk vetches, *Astragalus* species, that actually collect selenium and survive. These plants are often associated with a disease known as blind staggers that affects many grazing animals. A related genus, known as locoweed, *Oxytropis*, has similar properties. The disease name and the older common name locoweed indicate selenium's effect on animals as part of the poisoning process.

Silicon, a non-metallic element, is the second most abundant element in the earth's crust. The sands found throughout a good portion of the world contain a large proportion of silicon, and sandy soils can contain up to 40 percent of this element. A plant that is so common in North America that we do not need to travel far to visit an area where it grows is the weedy horsetails, *Equisetum* species. These plants thrive in moist to very wet sandy regions, spreading rapidly by creeping rhizomes, to the point of invasiveness. They have soft, fine and airy foliage. Horsetails absorb silica and are so full of it that the plants have been used as abrasive pot scrubbers.

These examples give you a good idea of how remarkably some plants can adapt to their chemical environment.

169

CHAPTER THIRTEEN

FIRE AND PLANTS

In 2009, a devastating forest fire encroached upon the city of Kelowna, British Columbia, destroying over 200 homes, practically eliminating a large provincial park and threatening the edges of the city itself. It was a hot, arid summer, and the trees of the forest had not received any rain for quite some time and were tinder-dry. The fire evoked an eerie, frightening mood — you could actually see flames shooting from the tops of the trees and licking the sky. Although it was a cloudless day, the sky was darkened by black smoke tinted with the orange glow of fire, and the sun was a reddish-orange glowing ball with diminished light. Ash was falling all around, quite densely at times, and even chunks of charred bark and leaves would fall from the sky.

Although forest fires can pose extreme threats to our

170

homes, workplaces and our very lives, they are a natural occurrence. Fire clears the accumulation of forest floor debris, such as needles and dead branches, as well as overgrown undergrowth that can rob the soil of nutrients. Fire is a fresh start for the forest — many species of plants reestablish the forest by growing rapidly after a fire.

We love living close to the forest for the beauty, peace and serenity it provides, but man's presence has upset the balance of the forest ecosystem. We disrupt the natural cycle of many species of trees, which need periodic fires to reproduce and allow the species to continue. This disruption lets a huge amount of combustible material, living and dead, accumulate on the forest floor, far more than nature would permit. As a result, when a fire finally does occur — and humans are one of the main causes of forest fires, though most often inadvertently — it is usually with increased severity.

There are several man-made solutions to these concerns, including thinning the forest and putting up fire breaks — inserting an expanse of space between trees to prevent fire from spreading. Fire-resistant plants can also be established as barriers to help limit the spread of forest fires. While we are grateful to those who work for our forests and those who risk their lives as firefighters, we are also fascinated by the often amazing ability of plants to regenerate themselves by adapting to and sometimes even surviving forest fires.

171

FIRE-DEPENDENT PLANTS

Many plants are actually dependent on fire to release their seeds for reproduction and continuation of the species. Here we address many of these remarkable plants and their fire-adaptive survival strategies.

We start with some of the fire-dependent pines, *Pinus* species, that need the heat of fire to open their cones and release their abundant seeds. These include the Monterey pine, *P. radiata*; bishop pine, *P. muricata*; knobcone pine, *P. attenuate*; and the jack pine, *P. banksiana*. The lodgepole pine, *P. contorta*, forests that cover a good portion of British Columbia may retain their closed cones for up to 50 years, just waiting for the heat of a forest fire to release the seeds. Sometimes very hot weather will be enough to encourage the cones of some pine species to release their seeds, accompanied by snapping or crackling sounds. You may have noticed that seeds from the cones of pine Christmas trees sometimes shoot across the room when fried by indoor heat.

Another giant conifer of the northern coast of California whose cones need the heat of a forest fire in order to release seeds is the giant sequoia, *Sequoiadendron giganteum*. These majestic trees may keep their cones tightly shut for decades, to open only when heated to 120°F or higher — temperatures that can be achieved only by the intense heat of a forest fire.

The Monterey cypress, *Cupressus macrocarpa*, of the

172

Callistemon citrinus, bottlebrush NEAL KRAMER

central California coast is another example of a conifer that requires the heat of a forest fire to open its seed capsules.

Although not often thought of as cone-bearing plants, *Banksia* species have their seeds enclosed in relatively large cones. These cones remain tightly closed, releasing their seeds only in forest-fire conditions. Many *Banksia* species also have the ability to regrow from the base after a wildfire. Rather than visiting after a fire, let's observe these plants in flower, down in Australia. During our long hike across much of the country, we are fortunate to have observed several different species, each with exquisitely colored, densely packed flower spikes.

During our travels in Australia, we also come across many beautiful, often scarlet-flowered bottlebrush, *Callistemon* species. These evergreen shrubs or small trees sport spectacular clusters of red flowers tightly concentrated

173

at the ends of cylindrical spikes. Though their seed capsules are not cones, they are woody, and like those of *Banksia*, their seeds are not released until there is a wildfire.

Still in Australia, we are also privileged to observe many cycad species. These remarkable plants often bear huge cones that require a fire to release the seeds stored within. Some species even need fire to stimulate the production of these cones. Several species of *Cycas* are well known for producing abundant seeds after being burned and are well adapted to resisting fire. Even though the aboveground portion of the plants may be charred, leaf bases that cover the trunk often remain as additional protection from fire. Also from the base, new growth usually emerges rapidly after a fire, and the plants fully recover from the ordeal.

We also observe many of the fire-prone *Eucalyptus* species, most of which depend on fire to reproduce and spread. Wildfires clear the forest floor of competing shrubs and tree seedlings, allowing *Eucalyptus* seedlings to reforest. In the case of species like the towering Australian Mountain Ash, *E. regans*, this clearing of the forest floor is imperative. Although mature trees here are killed by a forest fire, the only means for these trees to reproduce is from seeds that are released and dispersed only under such conditions. Either way, all eucalypts are well known for their ability to reestablish themselves after forest fires, and usually rapidly.

Protea cynaroides, King protea ROBBIN MORAN

We now head to South Africa to observe their national flower, the King protea, or sugarbush, *Protea cynaroides*. In spring, the King protea bears many spectacular gigantic 10-inch flower heads. They are shallow and bowl-shaped, pink and snowy white tinged with yellow. Once these flowers have been pollinated and have set seed, they become covered by bracts that consist of a tough asbestos-like fiber that protects the seeds inside. These bracts will not open until exposed to the heat and flames of a bush fire. Only then are the seeds released to ensure regeneration of the species.

Our travels next take us to the Mediterranean, specifically a hot, dry summer area near the south coast of Spain. Here we find several beautiful species of the rockrose, *Cistus*, with their often pristine white petals and yellow-centered

175

Haemanthus coccineus, a fire lily DAVID NIXON

blooms. The particular species we are looking for is *C. salvifolius*, and we are not disappointed. The attractive plants we come across are short shrubs with soft sage-like foliage covered with white and yellow-centered flowers. The seeds of these rock roses have an extremely hard outer coat that must be ruptured by the heat of a wildfire before they can germinate.

FLOWERING AFTER FIRES

There are several plant species, including many bulbous plants, that flower only after a forest fire — or, in some cases, flower more profusely after a fire. Of particular interest here are certain appropriately named fire lilies, such as *Cyrtanthus ventricosus*. We find these on a south-facing sandstone slope in the fynbos of South Africa. These bulbous plants, related to the amaryllis, have carpeted the landscape with their exquisite bright red nodding flowers a mere nine days after a fire has passed through the area.

176

Xanthorrhoea glauca ssp. *angustifolia*

This is a welcome sight, as fire lilies only flower almost immediately after a forest fire has burned itself out and cooled. Shortly after the plants have flowered, they set — make ready for germination — and release seed. These fire lilies may not flower again for 20 years, usually after another fire has passed through the area.

Other fire lilies of the South African fynbos that we observe are species of *Haemanthus*, including the impressive red-flowered *H. coccineus*, pushing its way up out of a rock outcropping.

We next journey through the bushland of Australia to discover grass trees, *Xanthorrhoea* species, that are often conspicuous in the landscape after bush fires. Following a recent wildfire, we find several of these grass trees, the leaves at the base of the mature plants burned away, leaving scorched trunks. Soon the singed black trunks will develop long green reed-like leaves. These leaves are densely packed together,

177

Xanthorrhoea johnsonii M. FAGG © AUSTRALIAN NATIONAL BOTANIC GARDENS

and eventually they form a crown of foliage. Not long after the wildfire passed through the area, this same group of plants produced tall woody flower spikes, each profusely covered with small white flowers. The tallest of the species that we have observed is *X. arborea*, which can attain heights of up to 20 feet. We appreciate the scene, for grass trees bloom most prolifically after a wildfire.

178

Epilobium angustifolium (syn. *Chamerion angustifolium*) carpeting a hillside after a fire ALFRED COOK

After a long and enjoyable stay in Australia, we fly to the Yukon Territory in northern Canada, not far from Alaska. Few other cars are on the road as we travel along the east-west highway from Whitehorse. Ahead of us, to the right, we see an absolutely breathtaking scene that compels us to stop and linger. Unfortunately none of us has a camera, but this vista will stay etched in our memory for a long time.

179

The field before us was once a dense coniferous forest, but now all that remains of the trees are burned-out blackened stumps after the ravages of a forest fire. We are fortunate to have arrived near the end of the day, for this once-great forest has been replaced by a beautiful dense carpet of pinkish-purple fireweed, *Chamerion angustifolium* (syn. *Epilobium angustifolium*). The low angle of the sun in early autumn, just before sunset, intensifies the brightly colored flowers that stand against a background of darkened forest. As its name suggests, fireweed usually blooms prolifically after a forest fire.

Often there is a good reason why plants are given their common names. The fire willow, *Salix scouleriana*, and the fire or pin cherry, *Prunus pensylvanica*, are excellent examples. Each of these plants is so named because their seedlings rapidly occupy areas that have been burned out after a forest fire.

PLANTS THAT ARE FIRE-RESISTANT

Many plants have developed means to either survive forest fires, or at least give their progeny the best possible chance to survive. Most deciduous trees and shrubs are fire-resistant to varying degrees because of the high moisture content in their leaves. Fire-resistant plants have one or more of the following characteristics:

- leaves are moist and supple;
- plants have little dead wood and do not accumulate dry, dead material;
- sap is water-like and does not have a strong odor;
- no volatile oils or waxes in the leaves;
- high salt content in the leaves;
- thick layer of insulating bark.

To discover one of the most fire-resistant plants in the world, we travel to a highly alkaline desert soil region of California. Here we find what we are searching for in a collection of the gray- to silvery-foliaged fourwing saltbush, *Atriplex canescens*, scattered in tumbled mounds across this otherwise barren, sandy landscape. All species of *Atriplex* are fire-resistant and found throughout the temperate and subtropical zones, but especially the central and western United States and the dry interior of Australia. Although *Atriplex* species may be scorched and blackened by fires, little other damage is done and these plants come back as healthy as before. They are also heat- and drought-tolerant and effective for erosion control. For these reasons, as well as for their fire resistance, new cultivars of *Atriplex* are sure to be developed.

We remain in California to observe another well-known fire-resistant plant, the perennial succulent ice plant, *Carpobrotus edulis*, or the Hottentot fig. Though originally native to the coast of South Africa, this ice plant was widely introduced to areas such as California, Australia, southern Europe and portions of South America for erosion control and landscaping purposes. The plant's extremely aggressive and invasive nature has often choked out native plants in these areas. Ice plants spread rapidly, both by seed and extensive creeping, dense mat-forming stems that root easily.

Atriplex canescens, fourwing saltbush STEVEN PERKINS

As well, several different animals eat the fruits, helping to widely disperse its seeds. Ice plants are very salt-tolerant, both to salinity and salt spray from the ocean, as well as to moist coastal and dry interior regions. As you can see, ice plants are very tough.

It is a shame such tough plants are so invasive, for their ability to adapt to difficult situations is admirable. Further, the ice plants are incredibly beautiful. The large expanse of plants we find are sprawled across this sandy beach. Their satiny daisy-like flowers are blooming profusely. These open pale yellow at around noon each day and age to pink or light purple. The carpet of blooms seems to glisten in the bright sunshine — a spectacular display! The foliage also glistens in the sun, because the rich green leaves are covered by soft silvery hairs that give a grayish-blue ice-crystal appearance. The flowers are followed by edible fig-like fruits.

Carpobrotus edulis, hottentot fig NEAL KRAMER

Other attractive fire-retardant species include *C. acinaciformis*, *C. aequilaterus* and *C. roseus*, each with glistening purple flowers.

There is a report from many years ago, that in California, one single home remained unscathed by a fire that destroyed 150 other homes. The owner attributed the survival of his home to the many ice plants and cacti surrounding the structure as a groundcover — these species have high moisture content, and some also have high salt content. As this report suggests, fire-retardant species can be used in barrier plantings to help limit the spread of forest fires and protect homes and other structures against damage in fire-prone areas.

Several species survive fires by underground roots or tubers that regenerate the plant after the danger has passed. Many species of cycad, for example, have seedlings that develop from blackened stems that grow from the apex below the soil surface. This protects the plants from the frequent droughts and fires that occur in Australia, South Africa and Central America, where cycads are predominantly found.

Many species of the fire-prone eucalypts also regenerate quickly after a forest fire, sprouting from buds under the bark of blackened trunk stumps. These same plants have woody tuberous roots that enable them to survive both fire and drought by rapidly regrowing.

Carpobrotus edulis carpeting a seashore cliff NEAL KRAMER

Certain low-growing cacti, such as *Discocactus* species, survive the frequent savannah fires in their native Brazil by sprouting new growth from their underground root system. These cacti also utilize the cooler air found near the soil surface after a fire has passed.

Tamarix species usually grow in dry areas of North Africa, Southern Europe and temperate Asia, with many

185

introduced to other regions of the world. They are fairly fire-resistant because of their deep taproots, and likely because of their uncommon ability to absorb and store salt.

Several species of African coral tree, *Erythrina*, are very fire-resistant as well. These fascinating trees and shrubs, often with thorny stems, usually display flamboyant scarlet flowers.

Although not associated with surviving wildfires, there is one plant we must visit in the Mediterranean for some of its amazing traits. Most often referred to as the gas plant, though sometimes as the burning bush, *Dictamnus albus* is a beautiful and unique perennial. We are initially taken by the spikes of fragrant white to pinkish flower clusters and finely toothed light green leaves. Then, as we rub the leaves gently, a delightful lemon-peel scent is released. Now we do something unusual that we have been told is safe and demonstrates why the plant has earned its common names. The whole plant, particularly the older flowers, is covered with oil glands that emit a strong, spicy fragrance. So much oil is produced, in fact, that on hot, windless summer days such as this, the excess oil turns to vapor that can be ignited by a match — so a member of our party lights a match close to a plant. This is perfectly all right, as you will see. The bush is briefly engulfed in flames, amazingly without suffering any damage.

186

Dictamnus albus, burning bush
DR. AMADEJ TRNKOCZY

TREES WITH FIRE-RESISTANT BARK

We now visit several forested regions of the world to observe trees with thick fire-resistant bark, and we learn a bit about their habitat and other traits.

We travel first to coastal northern California to enjoy the magnificent towering California redwood. Upon entering the forest here, we are awestruck by the sheer size of the giants towering above us. These beautiful trees are some of the tallest in the world. Perhaps not well known is that these lofty giants also show remarkable resiliency and resistance to forest fires. This is mainly because of a thick, fibrous, highly attractive reddish-brown outer bark that is soft and spongy, containing little to no resin. These attributes have allowed the California redwoods to survive relatively unscathed for countless years, while other species of trees have been consumed by forest fires. Some of the redwoods

187

Sequoia sempervirens, California redwoods

have been scorched and burned deeply, yet even these continue to survive.

In the same vicinity we find a close cousin of the California redwoods in the giant sequoia. The bark of these huge trees is similarly thick, often deeply furrowed, with an attractive reddish-brown outer bark. The spongy outer layer of bark may be 12 to 18 inches thick, and up to 2 feet thick near the base of older trees. This bark is almost as effective as asbestos in resisting fire. The trees also contain tannic acid, a natural chemical once used in fire extinguishers, and the tree's sap is water-based, further increasing its resistance to fire. Branching usually starts way up, at nearly 200 feet from the ground — we must stretch our necks back to see the forest canopy high above. This provides the trees with even further protection, as the foliage is so far from the fires that may rage below.

Hiking inland to a more mountainous region, we find the incense cedar, *Calocedrus decurrens* (syn. *Libocedrus decurrens*). Although young trees here often succumb to forest fires because of their thin bark, resinous content and aromatic oils, mature trees — with their thick layer of protective bark — usually survive.

Traversing to a mountainous region of southern California, we find the big cone Douglas fir, *Pseudotsuga macrocarpa*. These trees recover from fire damage by vigorously sprouting new growth quickly from scorched trunks and branches. It is ironic that

Sequoiadendron giganteum, big tree DR. AMADEJ TRNKOCZY

fire-suppression efforts in the areas where this tree grows allow large quantities of combustible materials, such as twigs and branches, to accumulate on the forest floor. This accumulation increases dramatically over the course of many years, creating the risk of more severely destructive and intense fires than if nature were allowed to take its course. The majority of Douglas fir species around the world have protective bark, up to 12 inches thick, that is often reddish brown, deeply furrowed into scaly ridges and sometimes corky in texture. The Douglas fir relies on forest fires for its survival, for fire clears the ground around the bases of the trees so seedlings can take hold and eliminate competition from other tree species, because of the speed with which they grow.

We travel north now, to inland British Columbia, to observe the most fire-resistant tree in the region, the western larch, *Larix occidentalis*. These narrow deciduous conifers grow tall with horizontal branches that start spreading high above us. They often boast outstanding autumn foliage color. The western larch follows or survives fires, often later replaced by other tree species that grow more quickly. These trees have a reddish-brown bark with many overlapping plates and are often deeply furrowed. The outer bark layer can be as thick as 10 to 18 inches on older trees.

PLANTS THAT ARE FIRE-PRONE

Plants that are prone to fire have some of the following characteristics, in contrast to that of the fire-resistant plants:

- leaves are aromatic;
- plant contains volatile waxes or oils;
- sap is gummy, resinous and strong-colored;
- bark is loose, thin or papery;
- dead wood and dry material accumulate within the plant;
- root systems are shallow.

Let us consider a selection of these fire-prone plants. First we do a bit of globetrotting to have a look at several coniferous fire-prone pines, *Pinus*; spruce, *Picea*; and *Thuja* species. We don't have to travel far for our first example, for many cedar, *Thuja* species, are used as a hedging material by people in temperate regions of the world. These trees have a thin layer of loose, almost papery bark that peels or sheds easily. The sap is gummy and resinous, with a strong dark honey coloring. The trees are shallow-rooted, requiring extra water — definitely not a tree for hot, dry areas for this reason alone. The trees also have plenty of accumulated dry, flammable leaf and twig debris both within and

191

at the base. Moreover, the aromatic leaves contain volatile waxes and oils. From this, you can see that cedars meet all of the characteristics of a highly fire-prone plant. So why are cedars planted as hedging material, especially in areas with hot, dry summers and the potential for forest fires? The answer is possibly because cedars grow fairly quickly. Forestry services in many regions recommend that cedar trees used as hedging material should be planted a minimum of 30 feet from houses and other structures. Why not plant more fire-resistant plants instead?

Pines and spruce species are found throughout the world, so we don't have to travel far to find them. Many of these trees have a highly flammable resinous content in their foliage and thin bark, gummy and strongly colored sap, aromatic foliage and often accumulated dry material in the trees themselves and on the forest floor.

Next we head to Australia and vicinity, where we encounter some of the most flammable trees on earth, the eucalypts, *Eucalyptus* species. The majority of eucalypts contain extremely high levels of flammable oils. On hot summer days, some of this highly aromatic oil vaporizes, causing a bluish haze over the forest. A contender for the world's tallest tree, the stately mountain ash eucalyptus, *Eucalyptus regans*, has wood so impregnated with volatile oils that these forests are a natural fire hazard. It is said that so much oil is present that flames could shoot great distances into the sky, up to 300 feet. Another common species, the Tasmanian Blue Gum, *E. globulus*, has peeling bark that accumulates on the forest floor, increasing the fire hazard.

Our journey now takes us to arid regions of western North America, east of the Cascade mountains. We first come across many tumbleweed plants, *Salsola kali*, rolling across the dry, dusty landscape in their loose balls of branches, reminding us of ghost towns in western films. Originally from Eurasia and now well-established here, these weeds, although heat- and drought-tolerant, are also highly flammable. Another plant introduced to this same region and habitat, originating from Western Europe and North Africa, is the gorse or furze, *Ulex europaeus*. These spiny shrubs with bright yellow flowers and dry branches contain a great deal of oil, making the plants a real fire hazard by roadside forested areas or homes. If you can endure cutting and collecting the thorny branches, gorse does make an excellent fuel for starting a campfire. One more highly flammable plant of this same region, often found in areas even too dry for sagebrush, is the antelope bush, *Purshia tridentata*. Also known as greasewood, it is filled with very flammable oils. The tall, rigidly branched, sparsely spread group of plants we've found have silvery greenish hairy foliage. Greasewood also makes an excellent fuel for the campfire.

193

Many Mediterranean plant species, such as rosemary, sage and thyme, contain aromatic oils that help protect these plants against water loss in heat and drought. However, these same oils are also highly flammable and could exacerbate the spread of fire.

We cannot leave the subject of fire-prone plants without mention of one of the largest plant families in the world:

Ulex europaeus, gorse or furze VIRGINIA SKILTON

the grass, *Gramineae*, family. All one needs to do here is think of the grass or savannah fires that often rage across huge expanses of dry regions of the world, especially in Australia or Africa.

Although we love to live near the beauty of the forest, we must also consider that many of the trees there are dependent upon fire. Our insistence on suppressing the natural cycle of forest fires actually increases the intensity and danger of fires when they do occur, upsetting the natural cycle of the environment. We must learn to live in harmony with the forest.

195

CHAPTER FOURTEEN
RAIN FORESTS

There are three very broad categories of trees, based on latitude: tropical, temperate and boreal. Our focus here is on tropical and temperate zones, for these are where rain forests are found. A rain forest is simply a forest that receives large amounts of rainfall each year: where rainfall is spread throughout the year, most plants are evergreen, whereas where rainfall is seasonal, plants may be evergreen or deciduous.

TROPICAL RAIN FORESTS

Most rain forests are found in tropical regions, including Central America, West Africa, Southeast Asia and Australia. Here, rainfall is fairly constant and year round. The high humidity and high temperatures promote rapid and prolific

196

plant growth. There are no definable seasons in the forest, so whatever the time of year, you will find some trees and plants in flower and some in fruit. An amazing number of plant species grow in tropical rain forests, more than in the rest of the world combined.

The tropical Daintree Rainforest on the northeast coast of Queensland, Australia, is well worth a visit. This lush forest region has incredibly beautiful scenery that often features sandy beaches. It is the largest continuous area of tropical rain forest on the continent.

South America's Amazon rain forest comprises over one half of the world's rain forests. The vast, lush growth of the Amazon rain forest covers over 2.1 million square miles. Mostly situated in Brazil, it also stretches into eight other countries. If you look at a satellite image, you will see how huge this lowland evergreen rain forest region is.

The Amazon rain forest is immensely important as it boasts the greatest diversity of plant species in the world. A recent account has registered 438,000 species of plants in the region — not including many more species not yet discovered or catalogued. Unfortunately, because of intensive clearing for timber and agricultural and urban development, much of this treasured rain forest is quickly disappearing. This major ecological and environmental concern affects not only the survival of many plant species, but that

197

of animals, insects and microorganisms as well. Thankfully, in many areas, governments are placing these tropical rain forests under protection by law, and they are setting aside large tracts of land to establish special reserves — actions intended to help save the Amazon rain forests.

Now let us have a closer look at the Amazon rain-forest region, keeping in mind that many of our observations are applicable to other tropical rain forests as well. Upon entering the Amazon, the first thing you might notice is how high the tree canopy is above you. The majority of these towering trees have slender trunks that branch only near the top. The canopy is so dense with leathery evergreen foliage that most of the sun's light is blocked from reaching down to the forest floor and understory plant life. As a result, only plants that can survive in permanent twilight conditions are found at the base of the trees. The tropical rain-forest floor is actually fairly open and easy to walk through. This is in stark contrast to how we often picture a tropical rain forest — as an impenetrable jungle that one would require a machete to travel through. In fact, this type of undergrowth occurs only in open areas, such as along riverbanks or in clearings created by fallen trees, where sunlight can reach the forest floor.

The tree trunks are wet here and the ground is soggy. The canopy overhead is so dense that you might not be able

198

to tell whether the water constantly trickling down is from rainfall or condensation falling from the treetops.

Although plant life is prolific, mainly because of ideal temperature and moisture, it may be surprising to some that the soil is actually quite poor here. This is precisely because of these ideal conditions, for the organic matter is quickly decomposed, with nutrients rapidly taken up by the trees and other plants. As a result, almost all the nutrients are locked up within the bodies of living organisms, leaving little organic matter in the soil.

From an environmental standpoint, when a tropical rain forest is cut down, the exposed soil has little humus to retain moisture and nutrients. With no more trees or plants left, the little soil that remains is washed downstream by the region's heavy rainfall. Such cleared land rapidly loses fertility and leaves a very shallow soil layer, making for unproductive farmland.

Many of the trees here have huge buttressed trunks and snaky roots to help support them in the shallow soils. Because the organic-matter layer on the rain-forest floor is extremely thin, most of the trees spread their roots widely, but not deeply into the ground.

These forests are also home to considerable mosses and lichens and, higher up, many beautiful epiphytic plants, such as orchids, bromeliads and ferns. Many of the ferns

199

produce their own soil way up in the forest canopy, by trapping dust and organic matter that will hold water as well as provide nutrients. Lianas of all sorts are clambering up and over tree branches and trunks, and other plants benefit from this as well. These vines have their roots in the soil but are supported by the giant trees they climb on and around. It's a botanist's dream environment, for plant life abounds wherever one looks.

TEMPERATE RAIN FORESTS

Temperate rain forests occur in climates near the sea or ocean, where there is abundant winter rainfall and temperatures are mild. In summer, these regions are dry and cooler with considerable cloudiness or fog, which provides the moisture necessary to sustain plant life. These forests are home to many of the largest living things on earth, such as the California redwoods and giant sequoia or big trees of northern California.

Temperate rain forests are found in areas such as the mixed coniferous forest of the Olympic Peninsula of Washington State, the wettest place in the continental U.S.; Cathedral Grove on Vancouver Island in British Columbia; and many other regions.

In temperate rain forests, plants grow in practically every last inch of space. The forest floor here is covered with a thick spongy layer of rich organic mulch, even though the soil is shallow. This ground cover and the considerable moisture in these forests create an ideal environment for lush green growth. Tree branches are covered with mosses and lichens and epiphytic plants, while the understory is carpeted with ferns and other smaller shade-loving plants.

CLOUD FORESTS

Imagine traversing a high coastal mountain region of western South America, where all around you is lush, dense foliage and tall trees, and everything in sight is shrouded in a dense fog that permeates the air with moisture. The rugged, lofty mountainous terrain holds the mist-laden air mostly in the forest canopy, providing abundant moisture for all that grows here. We are right in the clouds, and all the plant life here depends on these clouds, much more so than rainfall. Compared to the hot, humid lowland rainforest region, the air here is cooler but still humid.

So much condensation collects on tree leaves that much of this drips down to the undergrowth far below. Bright green moss covers tree trunks and the forest floor, with lichens draping gracefully from tree branches. Higher above, conditions are ideal for the many epiphytes and other moisture-loving plants, such as exotic orchids, bromeliads and tree ferns. The dense carpet of understory plants

201

grows in a leafy, humus-rich soil. It is protected from both wind and sun, being better adapted to the shade or dappled sunlight at this level of the forest, parts of which could be called moss forests, because of the abundance of mosses present.

Such cloud forests generally occur in mountainous terrain at about 2,300 to 9,850 feet. Important areas where cloud forests are found include Central and South America, east and central Africa, Indonesia, Malaysia, the Philippines, Papua New Guinea, the Caribbean, parts of Yukashima Island in Japan, the northern pacific coast of the U.S. and parts of both Australia and New Zealand.

CHAPTER FIFTEEN
TROPICALS

The word *tropical* brings to mind dense jungles of foliage or warm, sunny, sandy ocean beaches with palm or coconut trees overhead, cooled by a gentle breeze. While in some instances this may be true, tropical regions are much more diverse than this. The tropics, comprising the regions between the Tropic of Cancer and the Tropic of Capricorn latitudes, are characterized by a mostly hot, humid climate with varying amounts of rainfall, dependent on environmental and climatic factors in each region. The average year-round temperature in tropical regions varies, but generally averages out to around 68°F. Freezing temperatures are virtually unheard of, except in some areas that are farthest from the equator.

Although we have already covered tropical rain forests,

which constitute a large portion of the tropics, there are other extensive tropical regions — tropical seasonal forests, dry forests, grasslands, savannah, mountains and even deserts. With such diversity comes a corresponding diversity of tropical plant life.

Several regions of the tropics also experience pronounced wet and dry seasons. Areas of western Madagascar are a great example of a dry forest area — the plant life here has a lower canopy with fewer epiphytes but more climbing plant species. In contrast, the Atlantic forest of Brazil exemplifies the moist coastal forest. Other regions, such as Hawaii and New Caledonia, boast both moist and dry forests. Endemic plant species abound in each of these areas.

Tropical seasonal forests generally have lower canopies, with the proportion of deciduous trees expanding as precipitation decreases and the length of the dry season increases.

Tropical seasonal forests include the monsoon forests of India and areas of Southeast Asia, sometimes referred to as a tropical wet climate. Monsoon forests are a type of tropical deciduous lowland forest that grows in hot, humid regions with heavy seasonal rainfall. When the dry season comes to an end, and the monsoon winds and rains arrive, many of the trees here will open their leaves.

There are also subtropical regions that not only have rain forests, but also grasslands, savannah, mountains and deserts. In other words, the subtropics also have great diversity both in their climate and their plant life. They comprise the regions between the Tropic of Cancer and approximately 40° north latitude and also between the Tropic of Capricorn and approximately 40° south latitude. This zone is characterized by having both a wet and a dry season. An example here is the Mediterranean, with its wet winter and dry summer. Other subtropical regions may have a wet summer and a dry winter. The average year-round temperature in the subtropics varies, but it averages around 50°F for most of the year and 41°F during the colder months. It is uncommon for freezing temperatures to occur through much of the subtropical zone.

You will note from the preceding that arbitrary lines (latitudes) and zones for tropical and subtropical regions are man's attempts to simplify much more complex matters.

CHAPTER SIXTEEN

AQUATIC AND MARGINALLY AQUATIC PLANTS

When speaking of plants, aquatic simply means living or growing in or near water, in wetland regions such as bogs, marshes, fens and swamps. Plants here may be free-floating, totally submerged or rooted on the bottom with their leaves and flowers showing above the surface.

Bogs are most often associated with peat, and plants that grow in peat bogs are adapted to the high acidity in these bogs. The watery soil here is poor in nutrients and acidic to levels that would be toxic to most other plants.

Plants that require permanently moist conditions, ranging from mud to water, are considered marginally aquatic. The shallow waters at the sides of watercourses, such as rivers, streams and creeks, are called riparian wetlands.

Swamps, on the other hand, are usually dominated by trees, such as the mangrove, *Rhizophora* species, and related genera. These plants colonize wetlands, forming dense tangles of stilt-like roots (more about these in Chapter 11).

The swamps of western Florida consist mainly of swamp or bald cypress, *Taxodium distichum*, which have attractive, deeply fissured, fibrous reddish-brown bark.

Taxodium distichum, swamp cypress DANIEL L. NICKRENT

Nymphaea species, water lily NICKOLAY KURZENKO

Above the mucky, watery base of these giant cypress trees are what can only be described as knobby knees. These structures are vertical woody growths sent up from the tree's roots, allowing the tree to breathe while its roots are submerged under the water.

A pond in the same region might be home to the fragrant water lily, *Nymphaea odorata*. Our delightfully fragrant species opens its flowers early in the morning and closes them in the afternoon. This perennial aquatic grows from a thick, spreading rhizome with slender stems and attractive heart-shaped floating leaves. Each inflorescence of showy, intricately formed, many-petaled flowers is pristine white, pink or red.

The fragrant water lily can spread rapidly by underground stems breaking into pieces and by abundantly produced seed spread in the water. Although one of the most beautiful aquatic plants, they can grow into very dense

208

Calla palustris, wild calla ALFRED COOK

mats that inhibit the growth of other aquatic species by blocking the light. This species is found on lakes, ponds and slow-moving streams throughout central and eastern North America.

Usually found in marshy areas in the north central region of British Columbia, as well as throughout Alaska, the wild calla or water arum, *Calla palustris*, populates other similar wet areas of North America. These aquatic perennials have long creeping rhizomes by which they reproduce, and heart-shaped glossy dark green leaves. Each inflorescence consists of numerous yellowish-green flowers densely packed into a cylindrical spike, with a pure white bract enveloping the spike on one side. The flowers bring to mind the similar and related skunk cabbage arum, only on a much smaller scale and with white bracts rather than yellow.

After a brief hike on this island, we come to another

209

Nuphar lutea ssp. *Polysepala*, yellow pond lily ALFRED COOK

small lake, this time with a large grouping of the yellow pond lily, *Nuphar polysepalum*, floating on the shallow waters. We find this attractive and fascinating aquatic perennial has huge thickened rhizomes spreading laterally and either submerged or immersed. The large leathery heart-shaped leaves are also either floating or submerged. The solitary, large, waxy, cup- to bowl-shaped, floating bright yellow

Lemna minor, duckweed ALFRED COOK

inflorescences — reminiscent of a tulip — arise on long stalks from the rhizomes.

It is not uncommon to find thousands of specimens in the duckweed family, *Lemnaceae*, together in a small lake. Each plant consists of a single rounded leaf. The duckweeds, including this species, increase dramatically by budding into huge numbers of plants.

211

The duckweeds are miniature floating aquatic plants found throughout the world, on still or slow-moving fresh water. These plants spread rapidly by forming dense mats of foliage, sometimes doubling the area they cover within two or three days. They rarely flower, but when they do they are the world's smallest flowering plants. Of the four genera and about 40 species, perhaps the smallest is *Wolffia* and the tiniest

Eichhornia crassipes, water hyacinth
LOUIS-M. LANDRY

of these is either *W. borealis* or *W. columbiana*. Each plant is a mere quarter-inch across. The common name for the duckweeds is fitting, for these tiny floating plants are often eaten by ducks.

Brazil, and many waterways of the tropics, is home to one of the more aggressive aquatic invaders in the world. The otherwise beautiful flowered water hyacinth, though native to Brazil, has now aggressively invaded many waterways in the tropics and subtropics. It is a scourge in some of these regions, clogging ponds, ditches and canals. Spreading mainly by rhizomes, this weed is free-floating with oval to round glossy green leaves, each atop spongy bladders that help the plants to float and roam. The beautiful large blue or mauve flowers with a yellow spot at the center are erect on short spikes. Flowering is prolific, with each bloom opening within two hours of sunrise and wilting by evening. If only its aggressive tendencies could be contained.

The giant or Amazon water lily, *Victoria regia* (syn. *V. amazonica*), lives up to its name. The giant water lily's huge floating leaves are almost exactly orbicular and can measure up to 6 feet in diameter, with a 2- to 4-inch-high upturned margin around its circumference. Each of these fascinating leaves has an intricate pattern of flattened girder-like ribs that radiate from the center, united by lesser cross ribs, with air spaces for flotation. With reinforcement strength like this, an Amazon water lily can support up to 200 pounds. It is not difficult to imagine children happily jumping from one leaf to the next.

A single Amazon water lily can produce 40 to 50 of these huge leaves in a season. In addition, the plants produce beautiful pink flowers. All these special attributes make it a popular choice in public gardens. The giant water lily is so perfect in symmetry and construction that architects in London, England, in 1851, used the design of the leaves

213

Victoria regia (syn. *V. amazonica*), giant or Amazon water lily KENNETH ROBERTSON

to make the cast-iron framework for the world-famous Crystal Palace.

Shifting to a less exotic plant, the humble perennial cat-tail, *Typha latifolia*, with its familiar cylindrical brown flower spikes and narrow green to grayish-green grasslike leaves, is found throughout North America in marshes, ponds and shallow, slow-flowing water.

214

Typha latifolia, cattail ALFRED COOK

The common reed, *Phragmites australis*, forms a dense colony around the edges of lakes. This floating perennial aquatic spreads quickly by underwater rhizomes or stolons and can be extremely invasive. The plant is found on every continent except Antarctica, along the shorelines of lakes (such as here), along the sides of streams, in shallow water and in other wetland areas.

The water lettuce, *Pistia stratiotes*, is a floating aquatic perennial that spreads rapidly by creeping submerged stems (stolons) forming dense mats on the surface. It spreads even further when broken-off fragments of the plants link with other plants.

Phragmites australis, common reed JESSE VERNON TRAIL

CHAPTER SEVENTEEN

DEFENSIVE STRATEGIES

Certain plants have developed ingenious ways to defend themselves from marauding creatures that look upon them as a food or water source. Some of the main survival methods include thorns, poisons, hiding and mimicry, each of which we will explore in turn.

THORNS

The first defensive strategy of plants that comes to mind is thorns. Thorns assume a great variety of shapes and sizes, and so do the plants that carry them. Many of these thorny plants are formidable and imposing, several are beautiful and all are fascinating. There are even thorn forests in India, Sri Lanka, Mexico, South America, Africa and elsewhere. Thorns have proven to be very effective in protecting plants

Echinocactus grusonii, golden barrel cactus

from thirsty or hungry creatures. Many plants, trees, succulents and cacti have thorns on their trunks and branches. A great number of these also have swollen trunks and limbs. The thorns help ensure that the often huge reservoir of water stored within these plants isn't plundered.

The golden barrel cactus, *Echinocactus grusonii*, for example, is beautifully symmetrical, and each of its deep ribs has brilliant golden-yellow three-pronged spines arranged uniformly along its length. These sharp thorns can easily penetrate the skin of any creature that may unwittingly brush past. It would be folly to try and get this plant's store of water. When in bloom, their bright yellow flowers are borne in a dense circle right at the top of the plant, like a crown.

A close relative of the golden barrel cactus, *Echinocactus polycephalus*, is also spherical and grows in tight clumps.

The ribbed gray-green stems are almost hidden by the many reddish-brown spines.

While several acacias are beautiful, many can also be highly invasive. Although these thorny trees and shrubs are found in warm climates, more than half grow in Australia.

In southern Africa, *Acacia erioloba* is named after animals that have found a way to avoid the vicious thorns this tree

Echinocactus polycephalus DR. AMADEJ TRNKOCZY

bears. This succulent tree has attractive ball-shaped bright yellow flowers in loose clusters.

In the matorral of central Chile, the very thorny *A. caven* has paired thorns at the base of each leaf. This tree is also quite beautiful, displaying its ball-shaped golden flower heads in spring.

Native to the hot, dry regions of southwestern North

Acacia caven, vicious thorns ZOYA AKULOVA-BARLOW

America is where the appropriately named catclaw acacia, *A. greggii*, lives. This imposing tall shrub to small tree has many branches, each covered with thick, sharp, hooked thorns. The cruel thorns of this acacia can inflict painful cuts to any animal or person that wanders too close.

Aralia elata, Japanese angelica tree NICKOLAY KURZENKO

Tourists to the open-field regions of southern Japan might have the chance to observe the native *Aralia elata*. In full bloom, this group of suckering upright deciduous small trees and shrubs displays tiny white flowers in large clusters. The foliage is appealing as well — large compound leaves with many small leaflets. The stems of these aralias are covered thickly with spines that warn any interested animals or humans.

The hawthorn, *Crataegus* species, as its name suggests, carries an abundance of thorns as a defense measure. Well known in many temperate regions of the world, in some

221

areas they are referred to simply as "thorns." *Crataegus mac-racantha* is native to Massachusetts. The common names for this species are long-thorned hawthorn and, perhaps even more appropriately, scimitar. Even the specific name means "large spined." This is the most formidable of the thorns, with each of its many thorns measuring up to 5 inches long.

222   A selection of other thorny plants of note that you

may want to have a look at includes several members of the *Ceiba* genus; *Pachira quinata*, a tree of Central America with very pronounced thorns on its trunk and branches; *Aciphylla horrida*, a perennial native to Australia and New Zealand, and known as the "horrid Spaniard" because of its sharp, narrow, lance-like foliage; and *Alluaudia procera*, the thorny succulent octopus tree of southern and south-western Madagascar.

POISON

As if thorns were not enough, some plants can be extremely cruel by combining them with poisons. One such plant is a member of the ginseng family, *Araliaceae*. But don't let the beautiful *Oplopanax horridus*'s charms deceive you! Native to swampy areas of western North America, this medium-to tall-sized shrub has attractive large maple-shaped leaves and scarlet fruit. Both the specific name *horridus* and the common name devil's club are appropriate, because every part of the plant's stems and leaves is covered with menacing protruding spines. These thorns can puncture the skin and at the same time inject a poison that causes swelling and extreme pain to any hiker or animal that has the misfortune of brushing against the plant.

One further cruel plant of the spurge family *Euphorbiaceae* that combines thorns with poison is *Hura crepitans*. This huge

223

tree, with its explosive seed capsules, has a buttressed trunk and branches that are usually covered with sharp spines. Every part of this tree is poisonous, and if anyone injures it, the milky sap it releases can cause severe inflammation and irritation if it comes into contact with skin.

The *Euphorbias* and closely related plants are perhaps some of the most poisonous in the world. They are succulents, predominantly of desert areas in the tropics and subtropics and mainly found in Africa. All have a corrosive milky sap or latex that acts as a strong irritant. Many species of *Euphorbia* have spiny stems, and most collect and store water in their stems and trunks, enabling them to survive long periods of drought.

One especially nasty species is *E. desmondii* of Nigeria. At one time in the 19th century, villagers planted these shrubs all around their village to create a tall impenetrable barrier. It would be folly if an invading army were to chop this plant's stems to attack the village, for the plants would then release a poisonous latex. The latex would not only blister the attacker's skin, but could cause blindness as well if it got into the eyes.

One close relative to the *Euphorbias* in Africa is known as dead man's tree, *Synadenium cupulare*, and for good reason. The latex is as poisonous and caustic as that of *Euphorbia ingens*. This tree is said to irritate the skin, eyes and mouth

224

Euphorbia ingens WILLEM FROST

of anyone who simply handles it. Natives believe that the tree lures people and animals toward it to kill them, and that the ground around the tree is white from the bones of dead animals. They say the tree is so poisonous that birds flying overhead will fall dead from the sky. Whether or not these beliefs are true, this definitely sounds like a tree to steer clear of.

225

Urtica dioica, stinging nettle, close-up of stinging hairs NEAL KRAMER

The plants of the *Urtica* genus often have stinging hairs on their leaves and stems. The Latin *uro* in the generic name actually means *I burn*, and if you've ever had the misfortune of brushing against these plants, you know the name fits. The familiar weedy stinging nettle, *Urtica dioica*, was originally introduced from Europe, but it is now widespread across much of North America. The plants are coarse, erect perennials from short to tall, with creeping yellow roots sometimes visible at the soil line. The ovate toothed leaves and the stems sport many bristly stinging whitish hairs, and when in bloom, their small green to yellowish-green flowers hang in pendulous clusters.

The stings from the plants' bristly hairs is said to feel like multiple tiny hypodermic needles injecting poison into one's bare legs. Inflammation and irritation follow quickly. Interestingly, the antidote to the stinging nettle's sting

226

almost always grows nearby. Dock plants, *Rumex* species, when rubbed on the affected area, are said to provide relief.

Mimosa pudica, sensitive plant RAVAN SCHNEIDER

There are so many plants that use poison as a means of defense that here we can only mention a few of the most noteworthy ones. Poisonous plants are usually sending the message "Don't touch" and we should heed their warning.

HIDING

Some plants defend themselves simply by hiding from danger. Perhaps the most exemplary species employing this defense is the well-known sensitive plant, *Mimosa pudica*. Although it is native to Brazil, it has spread far and even become a noxious weed in places like Hawaii. These mat-forming plants can even take over farmers' fields. Each plant has green fernlike leaves consisting of paired rows of many leaflets, giving it a delicate look. Some of the plants have fluffy pinkish-violet flower heads.

227

Grazing animals are sometimes attracted to this seemingly delectable meal, but as they attempt to eat the plants, they seem to simply disappear. As the grazers depart, the plants reopen their leaves and lift their branches, for the danger has passed. Within seconds of being disturbed, the sensitive plant had folded up its leaves and lifted its branches. A fascinating means of defense!

Lithops species, living stones JAMES M. CARPENTER

Some plants hide visually instead of physically, blending in with their surroundings. Perhaps the most exemplary plants that use mimicry as a means of defense are the living stones or pebble plants, living rocks and living granite plants of the *Aizoaceae* plant family. Most of these are the living stones, of which the *Lithops* genera are best known. As the common name implies, these remarkable plants closely resemble stones in their natural habitat. They vary in color to camouflage — they can be yellow, gray, blue, brown, orange or creamy white.

Lithops, typical of these plants, consists of a pair of extremely thick leaves fused together at the base, with a slit at the top. This slit may reach right down to ground level or be only a tiny hole, depending on the species. The plants hug the ground or embed themselves in the soil. The swollen succulent leaves are water reservoirs that help the plants survive their harsh arid habitat. Living stones are rarely if ever attacked, for creatures simply don't see them. The only things that can give them away are their often brilliantly colored daisy-like flowers, when these are in bloom.

Lithops are predominantly found in Namaqualand, South Africa. Other living stones are in genera such as *Argyroderma*, *Conophytum* and *Lapidaria*. The living rock, or living granite plants, *Pleiospilos*, of South Africa, are a little taller growing and spread more.

229

CHAPTER EIGHTEEN

OFFENSIVE STRATEGIES

Can you imagine a plant being on the attack? After all, their ability to move is restricted to growing and seeking light — for the most part, that is. However, here we visit several plants that are on the offensive as part of their survival strategies.

There are two broad main categories for plants on the offensive: carnivorous and parasitic. (Some might even include epiphytic and strangler plants under these categories, for many of these plants can choke their hosts to death; but strictly speaking, these plants are neither parasitic nor carnivorous.)

CARNIVOROUS PLANTS

It may surprise you, but there are 600 or so species of carnivorous plant species in the world. These specially adapted

230

plants often grow in poor soil conditions, so they need to supplement their nutrition by capturing live prey. Most often their victims are insects, though larger carnivorous plants can even consume small animals, such as mice and frogs. Some of these carnivorous plants move remarkably fast in making the capture.

These fascinating carnivores have adapted some ingenious ways to trap and consume their prey. The trapping methods include sticky plant flypaper, bladders with vacuums to suck insects in, pitchers or pots to lure prey in and even a kind of cage that snaps shut on the luckless victims.

The sundews, *Drosera*, are a genus of carnivorous plants that use flypaper-like means to catch their prey. In the wet swampy areas of northern North America, Europe and Asia, a large number of a pretty perennial can be found among the reeds and sedges. Sundew, *Drosera rotundifolia*, consists of mostly submerged basal leaves with sturdy stems that spread in all directions, topped by pale green spoon-like leaf blades. Growing on the surface of these spoons are long reddish blade hairs tipped with a sticky liquid that both attracts and traps insects. The sundews are considered passive flypaper traps, for the sticky-tipped hairs remain still when trapping insects.

An active flypaper trap, *Drosophyllum lustanicum*, is related to the sundews and makes its home in the dry coastal hills of

231

Drosera rotundifolia, sundew LOUIS-M. LANDRY

the European Mediterranean coast. The main difference is that this species first traps insects with the sticky hairs, then the leaves slowly roll up to hold the prey more securely. The plants receive most of their moisture from fog and winter wet, and in spring display bowl-shaped bright yellow flowers.

The aquatic bladderwort plants, *Utricularia vulgaris* ssp. *macrorhiza*, found in Asia and Europe, take a different tack. The bright yellow orchid-like flowers sway gently atop wiry stems, and beneath the water's surface they have many trailing stolons covered with feathery foliage and distinctive bladder structures on both the leaves and stems. Originally these bladders were thought to act as flotation devices for the plants, but research has disproved this — they are actually vacuums to suck insects in. The vacuum activity of

232

Uticularia vulgaris ssp. *macrorhiza*, bladderwort ALFRED COOK

the bladders is an extremely quick process. First, an insect brushes against trigger hairs that are connected to a trap door; the door is then mechanically triggered and sucks the prey and surrounding water into the bladder; once the bladder is full, the trap door closes, the insect is ingested and then the whole process starts over again.

Perhaps the best known and possibly most fascinating carnivorous plant is the Venus flytrap, *Dionaea muscipula*. They bloom with white-flowered clusters atop wiry stems, but the main attraction is the specially adapted leaves. Each leaf consists of two flattened lobes with stiff spikes around the outer margin. An insect, attracted to the nectar in the leaf glands, lands on one of the lobes, expecting a meal. Instantly the leaf lobes of the Venus flytrap fold together to enclose its

233

Sarracenia purpurea ssp. *gibbosa*, pitcher IAN GARDINER

unsuspecting victim — a jail complete with bars. Enzymes in the plant then digest the insect, a process that can take as long as ten days. The lobes will then reopen, with nothing but small fragments of the insect remaining, which are quickly blown away by the wind.

A further trapping method used by several carnivorous plants is pitchers or pots to lure prey in. Species employing this method are often referred to as pitcher plants. A few genera and species that come to mind are the American pitcher, *Sarracenia purpurea*; the cobra lily, *Darlingtonia californica*, with its lobster pot traps; and *Heliamphora* species of Venezuela and adjacent regions. A typical pitcher plant uses a trail of nectar guides to lure insects into the mouth of

234

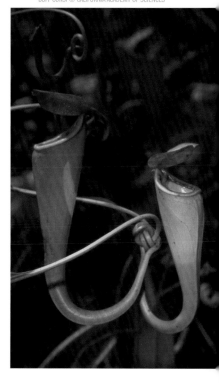

the pitcher. The inner surface of the pitcher is slippery, so the insect falls into the liquid in its base, unable to get out. Often the color and smell of the pitchers can also attract prey. The "lids" at the top of typical pitchers come in various sizes. The larger lids of certain species help to keep out rainwater that can dilute the digestive fluid inside.

A lobster pot pitcher, such as *Darlingtonia californica*, is a bit different in that this plant has a more pronounced funnel shape and hood, with a nectar-tipped tongue-like appendage to lure its prey. Once the insect enters the funnel-shaped pitcher, it can move in only one direction — special hairs force the insect down and into the pitcher.

Our representative genus of typical pitchers will be the remarkable *Nepenthes*. The majority of these species are found in the marshlands and tropical rain forests of

235

Southeast Asia. Many species can be quite beautiful as well as fascinating. For example, the intriguing *Nepenthes madagascariensis*, has a light yellowish pitcher with a reddish lid, and may have tendrils and display a rambling to liana-like lifestyle.

PARASITIC PLANTS

The other main category of plants on the offensive are the parasites, which supplement their nutritional requirements, either wholly or partially, directly from a host plant to which they attach themselves. There are a surprisingly large number of parasitic plants throughout the world. Certain species are entirely lacking in chlorophyll, while others are green leaved.

One of the first types of parasitic plants that come to mind are the mistletoes, which are often covered with lichen. These green-leaved parasites are different from many other parasitic plants, for they mainly attack the branches and upper parts of trees, whereas most other parasitic plants attack the roots and lower stems. You may ask how the mistletoes start their lives high in the canopy of the forest. Well, birds and climbing animal species eat the mistletoe berries and then disperse the seeds way up in the branches of the trees. The growing mistletoes penetrate

236

the host plants' branches and trunks to obtain nutrients. The mistletoes attach themselves to their hosts by suckers or haustoria, which are essentially modified roots. The roots of some species — such as the *Viscum* genus — actually grow within the tissues of their host plant.

There are many mistletoe examples, but perhaps the most familiar is the one that hangs over doors at Christmastime. One unique Australian mistletoe, known as the Western Australian Christmas tree, *Nuytsia floribunda*, may actually grow into a beautiful tree with abundant honey-scented yellowish-orange flowers. It flowers at Christmastime, hence the name. This tree usually gets its nutrients from the roots of grasses, but it will also parasitize the roots of any nearby plants, including pines — it's not fussy. This particular mistletoe species is a bit of an enigma, though, because when planted alone, it survives quite well without a host.

One remarkable parasitic plant is the toothwort, *Lathraea squamaria*. It is hidden under the ground most of the year, except April and May, in the moist, shady woodlands of Europe and central Asia. The plants push their flower shoots above the ground, revealing dull purple flowers clustered along each flower spike. When the flowers go to seed, the whole plant will die back to the ground once again.

237

Lathraea squamaria,
toothwort DR. AMADEJ TRNKOCZY

An examination of its underground growth habit reveals much-branched stems or rhizomes covered with thick, fleshy, scale-like leaves. These stems grow laterally in every direction, and some appear to be quite deep in the ground. These underground plant parts are whitish, indicating a total absence of chlorophyll. Where the toothwort roots meet up with the living roots of nearby trees, they fasten to the host tree or shrub roots quickly and then develop suckers at points of contact.

Plants are not toothwort's only victims: the cavities in the underground leaves can sometimes catch small burrowing animals that provide the plant with an additional source of nutrition. In other words, this widespread toothwort of temperate regions of Europe and Asia can live off of the juices of living host plants and, to a much lesser extent, the fluids of small animals.

238

Monotropa uniflora,
Indian pipe LOUIS-M. LANDRY

The Indian pipe, *Monotropa uniflora*, is totally white, entirely lacking chlorophyll. The waxy white stems with closely clinging white scale-like leaves are topped by tubular white flowers that droop to one side. This plant, which parasitizes the mycorrhizal fungus associated with the trees in the vicinity, is known as a saprophyte.

Another parasitic plant, this time from the meadows of Greenland, lives up to its intriguing name. From the deeply cut and feathery basal leaves of the elephant's head lousewort, *Pedicularis groenlandica*, emerge several flower spikes, each densely packed with pinkish-white to reddish-pink flowers. Each bloom unmistakably resembles an African elephant's head, complete with long floppy ears, a slender curving trunk and a small pointed mouth. You really are seeing pink elephants when you look at this plant!

239

Pedicularis groenlandica, elephant's head
lousewort VERNON SMITH

Although the specific name means *from Greenland*, the species actually has a very wide distribution, including east of the Cascade mountains in British Columbia. The elephant's head lousewort usually parasitizes certain grasses that grow nearby its moist to wet habitats.

CHAPTER NINETEEN

OTHER FASCINATING SURVIVAL STRATEGIES

This chapter is reserved for the best of the rest: special plant adaptations or characteristics that don't fall under the categories we've already considered.

CAN PLANTS TELL TIME?

There are certain plants that open and close their leaves at specific times. The morning glory, *Ipomea*, blooms prolifically, especially in the early morning. Before noon, all the flowers are closed. Chicory flowers, *Cichorium intybus*, which are so prevalent along many roadsides and in abandoned sites, open their exquisite vivid blue blooms in early morning and close at noon as well. Many of the evening primrose species, *Oenothera*, open their flowers in the late afternoon and remain open well into evening.

241

Some flowers open only in sunshine and close on dull days or whenever a cloud passes overhead. The four o'clock plant, also known as marvel of Peru, *Mirabilis jalapa*, opens its colorful trumpet-shaped blooms around — you guessed it — four o'clock each day. The flowers remain open until dark. On dull, overcast days the blooms open earlier and remain open all day.

The evening star, *Mentzelia decapetala*, opens its beautiful yellow flowers only after the sun goes down, perhaps because the evening star is pollinated by certain moths that visit at sunset and later. There are also two species of cactus that exhibit this nocturnal flowering habit. One, indigenous to Central America, is the queen of the night, *Hylocereus* species. These plants have large fragrant creamy-white flowers. The other nocturnal flowering species is *Selenicereus*, of tropical America and the Caribbean. *Selenicereus* have big, often fragrant, red or white flowers. These have evocative common names that include moon cactus, moon cereus and night-blooming cereus.

Perhaps the most amazing timekeeper plant is the evergreen Malayan shrub known as Simpoh, *Wormia suffruticosa*. Its flower buds begin to open at 3 a.m. Then the bright yellow flowers begin to open their petals at 3 a.m. the following day, and one hour before sunrise the flowers are fully open. At 4 p.m. of the same day, the petals fall, as each flower lasts only

242

a day. The resulting fruits, after pollination, take exactly five weeks to set. Pretty precise timing here, and this cycle continues, as the Simpoh flowers every day of its life.

DO PLANTS SLEEP *at* NIGHT?

The prayer plant, *Maranta leuconeura*, appears to sleep at night. During the day this fascinating plant's leaves are more or less horizontal. At night, however, the leaves fold together into an upright position as if in prayer. This plant also closes its leaves if placed in darkness, no matter what time of day it is, all within about 15 minutes. The prayer plant is also known as rabbit tracks or Ten Commandments because of the distinctive, often colorful markings on its leaves.

At dusk, many of us have observed the familiar clover of our lawns, *Trifolium repens*, raising and folding its leaves for the night. This clover is sometimes referred to as

Maranta leuconeura,
prayer plant JESSE VERNON TRAIL

shamrock and is probably the plant associated with the song "I'm Looking Over a Four Leaf Clover," even though the plant usually has only three leaflets on each leaf. It is very rare (lucky?) indeed to find a four-leaf clover. The clover is a member of the pea or legume family, *Leguminosae*. The leaves of most members of this large family usually perform sleep movements at night. *Mimosa* (remember the sensitive plant?) and *Neptunia* species assume their sleep position when touched.

Plants, then, move in response to touch or a change in light. They display true sense perception of their environment! In the case of light sensitivity, many plants relax their leaves at night, when the life-sustaining sunlight is unavailable. From a scientific perspective, the internal water pressure in leaves decreases at night and cells lose their turgidity. As a result, foliage can relax and even droop. The next morning, when the sun reappears, the internal water pressure is increased, causing the leaves to lift again to carry on with the plant's day.

The exceptions to this process are the prayer plant and the clover. These plants demonstrate the physical power to raise their leaves against gravity and force them into a vertical position at night — presumably a defense mechanism to prevent evaporation of moisture from the leaves.

CAULIFLORY

Imagine a tree with gigantic round fruits hanging in clusters at its base. Such is the cannonball tree, *Couroupita guinensis*, of moist-soil regions of the Amazon. So impressive are these fruits — and their highly attractive flowers — that the plant is also grown as a botanical curiosity in other tropical regions.

The cannonball tree exhibits the habit known as cauliflory in botanical circles. The tree flowers from the old bark of its trunk, and later develops huge cannonball-like fruits that hang in clusters from string-like appendages all around the trunk and base. These fragrant blossoms are rather pretty, in shades of yellow or brilliant reds or oranges. The resultant

Couroupita guinensis,
cannonball tree GUSTAVO SHIMIZU

fruits, or cannonballs, are reddish brown and at least 4 to 8 inches in diameter. When the wind blows, these cannonballs on strings often bang against each other and can make quite a racket. These low-hanging fruits are able to attract seed spreaders that often cannot climb trees.

The largest fruit in the world is also found growing at the base of the tree. This is the jackfruit, *Artocarpus heterophyllus*, of tropical regions. Its huge pear-shaped fruit can weigh up to 50 pounds — even a 90-pound specimen has been recorded! The usual weight of the fruit is about 20 pounds, which is still enormous, and each can measure 1 to 3 feet long and 10 to 20 inches in diameter. If the fruit of this tree were to grow on the branches, the branches would surely break under such weight.

The breadfruit, *A. incise*, a close relative to the Jackfruit, has smaller yet still hefty edible fruit. The cauliflory habit of this tree certainly makes the picking especially easy. The breadfruit is associated with the fateful sea voyage of Captain Bligh and the mutiny on the H.M.S. *Bounty* — in that story, the crew learns that breadfruit cures scurvy.

Several fig trees, *Ficus* species, also exhibit cauliflory, including the sycamore fig, *F. sycomorus*, mentioned in the Nicodemus story in the Bible. Several *Durio* species of Southeast Asia also demonstrate the cauliflory habit.

246

WOOD THAT RESISTS DECAY

There are three trees that are noteworthy because of their resistance to decay. The first is the common alder, *Alnus glutinosa*, which is indigenous to Europe, west Asia and North Africa. This alder thrives in boggy areas, and its wood can resist decay practically indefinitely under water. The second is the Huon pine, *Lagarostrobus franklinii*, an evergreen conifer of Tasmania. The wood of this tree is exceptionally resistant to decay, mainly because it contains a natural preservative oil that protects the tree from both rot and insect attack. The third tree is *Fitzroya cupressoides*, of southern Chile and Argentina. This tree is so durable that buildings constructed from it in the 17th century remain standing, with little noticeable weathering. Some logs from this tree that had been buried for over 2,000 years were found to have resisted rotting and remained intact.

A SHADY PARK BENCH

Looking for a park bench to sit on and something to shield you from the hot sun in Argentina? Then the ombu tree, *Phytolacca dioica*, will meet your needs. This huge evergreen of the grass, high-rainfall pampas regions provides both the bench and the shade. What more could one ask for in a tree?

The ombu is massive — up to 60 feet tall, with a huge umbrella-like foliage canopy. It makes a wonderful shade

247

tree, as each of its great branches extend outward for up to 50 feet. The trunk appears swollen and the base of the tree can measure up to 90 feet in circumference, often with multiple trunks. Both the bark and the trunks frequently give the impression that they are melting or flowing from the main part of the tree, spreading all around and over the ground in what seems like a thickened continuation of the trunk. This apparent melting is actually an extension of the tree's trunk that spreads out and becomes gigantic surface roots that protrude well out of the ground. Often these extensions of the tree are high enough above the ground to provide natural benches to sit on with an extensive canopy to provide shade.

In nature, ombus often grow miles apart, making them true hermits in the plant world. This makes it next to impossible for pollination to occur between the trees.

Another fascinating trait of the ombu tree is that it is virtually unaffected by the grass fires that frequently occur in its native habitat, and therefore can be considered a fire-resistant tree. This is only when it is green, though, as its trunk and branches normally contain up to 80 percent water. However, if the tree has lost most of its moisture and is dry, due to prolonged drought, it is just the opposite and will catch fire as easily as a pile of newspapers.

The wood of the ombu is herbaceous, soft and spongy enough to be cut with a knife. Otherwise, the tree is

248

exceptionally tough and not affected in the least by insects or diseases. It is an extremely long-lived tree as well. The tree emits a foul odor at night, though this stench is not perceptible at all during the day. Beware, though, as the ombu's sap is highly poisonous.

COMPASS PLANTS

The tall, almost aristocratic compass or polar plant, *Silphium laciniatum*, of the American plains, has attractive deeply cut foliage and many bright yellow daisy-like flowers. True to its name, the opposite pairs of leaflets on the stem are all pointing north and south. Over the course of a full day, the leaf edges actually turn so that the flat leaf surfaces face away from the sun, while the leaf edges are in line with it. This is a defense mechanism to resist dehydration and help avoid the intensity of the hot sun, particularly the midday heat of a summer day. Another plant, also known as compass plant, or prickly lettuce, *Lactuca serriola*, a weed of North America, also displays these traits. If we were to head to Australia, we would find that a variety of broad-leaved evergreen trees also respond to the sun's heat in a similar fashion.

AMAZING BAMBOO

Imagine spending a serene night deep in the heart of one of China's bamboo-growing regions. You might be awakened just before dawn by loud squeaking and whining sounds. On warm, humid mornings, bamboo plants grow so incredibly fast that you can actually hear them growing — their stems and branches rubbing audibly against each other. This exceptionally fast rate of growth applies particularly to mature plantings. An old Chinese proverb puts things in perspective: "A bamboo tree grows six inches in the first

19 years and 20 feet in its 20th year. The best time to plant a bamboo tree is 20 years ago. The second-best time is now."

The fastest-growing plants in the world are bamboos belonging to the large and economically valuable grass family. Daily growth can be over 3 feet — nearly an inch and a half per hour — and after three months they can attain nearly 100 feet.

One further notable characteristic of many bamboo species is their widely spaced flowering periods, which can be anywhere from ten to 100

Bamboo JESSE VERNON TRAIL

years apart, or even more. Often, plants from the same genetic stock flower simultaneously, even though each is planted in a very different climate around the world. Some bamboo species die after flowering, which is especially sad given the long waiting period before they first flower.

JUST *for* FUN

If you wish to observe flowers opening naturally, then members of the common evening primrose family, *Onagraceae*, are among your best choices. The whole process, once started, can take only a few minutes. If you listen carefully, you can even hear the buds bursting into flower with a soft popping sound.

CHAPTER TWENTY

UNUSUAL SURVIVAL STRATEGIES

The key word for the survival strategies we explore here is *unusual*. Out of the ordinary or rare, often unique to a species or a very small number of species.

PLANTS THAT PRODUCE THEIR OWN HEAT

As incredible as it may sound, certain plants actually produce their own heat.

Native to North America, the skunk cabbage, *Lysichiton americanus*, is a plant known first and foremost for its scent. But it is a matter of personal opinion as to whether or not this aroma — intensified by contact with the foliage — is objectionable. The other common name for these attractive, intriguing perennials, swamp lantern, is more appropriate. Sunlight augments their already-brilliant golden-yellow flower

Lysichiton americanus, skunk cabbage LOUIS-M. LANDRY

spathes (bracts that enclose the flower), each of which stands erect and surrounds a spike of tiny yellowish-green flowers.

In early spring, when snow still covers the ground, a close observer may note that the snow is melted in circles around the base of each plant. You see, the swamp lantern can create its own heat to get a jump start on the season. The atmosphere around the basal growth of these plants

253

Soldanella alpina, Alpine snowbell DR. AMADEJ TRNKOCZY

may be 63°F higher than the surrounding air temperature.

In the European Alps, another plant can also heat things up: the incredibly beautiful Alpine snowbell, *Soldanella alpina*, with its exquisite cut-edged, bell-shaped mauve flowers atop wiry stems and a base of dark green leaves.

Another extraordinary example of heat generation in the plant kingdom is found in the Mediterranean and western Asia. The perennial *Arum orientale*, with a purplish spathe and fleshy arrow-leaved foliage, has been reported as having a temperature of about 109°F while the surrounding air was about 59°F. Remarkable!

One more heat-generating plant worth mentioning grows in the Negev Desert in southern Israel. There, a species of *Ramalina* can tolerate extreme air temperatures in the heat of summer, and yet it can also continue to photosynthesize when it is partly frozen. Known as lace lichen, this

Ramalina is essentially a combination of fungus and algae. It grows on a host tree without causing it any harm, requiring only sunlight and water to thrive. The plant will appear dead in the heat of summer, yet it will begin photosynthesis within a matter of seconds after receiving moisture.

RAIN TREES

Imagine standing or sitting under a tree and getting rained on, while outside the tree's canopy it is sunny and dry. While it may be hard to believe, several trees around the world have the amazing ability to produce their own rain. The best-known rain tree is *Samanea saman* (syn. *Albizia saman*), which is native to a wide region of northern South America and southern Central America and broadly cultivated elsewhere.

A member of the legume, *Leguminosae*, family, *Samanea saman* is one of those trees said to perform sleep movements at night. At night or in cloudy weather, the rain tree folds its diamond-shaped leaflets together and reopens them at dawn or when sunshine returns. This movement allows any rain that had collected in the tree's dense canopy during the night to fall to the ground.

Another viewpoint is that there is no sleep movement at all — at least not to any great extent. In this scenario, the *Samanea saman* is full with a dense expanse of foliage to help protect itself from the hot sun during the day. At night,

255

however, the tree is almost open to the sky, as it folds its multitude of leaflets upward against gravity, into tight vertical positions. To maintain this upright position takes considerable physical power, and hence the leaves are not performing sleep movements at all. In effect, the tree cannot relax its leaves until the sun returns and the leaves can once again open.

Further, the rain tree produces additional moisture through condensation. Some of the rain produced is water or honeydew excreted by certain sap-sucking insects. In addition, the nectarines on the leaf petioles of the tree may excrete a sugary juice to the ground below.

In any event, the grass directly under the canopy of the *Samanea saman* is usually much greener than the surrounding grass.

Samanea saman also has an extensive shallow root system to better absorb its self-produced rain. Several of its roots protrude from the ground and spread in a snake-like manner. Its extensive, extraordinarily wide, domed or umbrella-shaped canopy of foliage can be 100 feet across when the tree is fully grown, even when the average height of the tree is 50 to 80 feet. Obviously, considerable room is needed for this tree to grow to its full potential. The tree makes a dramatic, impressive and beautiful statement in the landscape, which is ample reason why it is grown so extensively outside of its native home.

Samanea saman, rain tree MYAATARO

EPHEMEREDES

In the desert regions of southwestern North America, a few bright yellow daisy-flowered desert marigolds, *Baileya multiradiata*, may be found poking out of rocky outcroppings. These beautiful little perennials bloom profusely atop wiry stems and above sparse yet attractive silver-gray foliage. Besides its toughness in the face of the arid climate

257

Baileya multiradiata var. *multiradiata*, desert marigold JAMES M. ANDRÉ

of its home here, the desert marigold has a further way to cope with adverse conditions in summer. You see, the plant is one of only a handful known as an ephemeral — a plant that can complete its full life cycle within a matter of weeks. If conditions are just right, an ephemeral can do this several times in one season. Under laboratory conditions, this plant can germinate, flower and set seed within three to four weeks. It must be a world record holder in this category.

PLANTS THAT GROW COMPLETELY UNDERGROUND

There is an orchid, *Rhizanthella gardneri*, in Western Australia that spends its entire life underground, buried in the soil. The underground orchid, as it is often called, has neither leaves nor roots and is incapable of producing chlorophyll for growth — even flowering takes place beneath the soil. The plant consists of a fleshy underground storage

258

stem or tuber that produces a flower head packed with up to 150 tiny blooms. The only time any part of the plant is exposed is when the flowers are ready to be pollinated — the flower heads from several plants emerge from the soil, forming small indentations in the ground. The indentations allow insects to enter and pollinate the blooming flowers even though they are still belowground. Once pollinated, the flowers again disappear into the soil.

The underground orchid is a parasite on the fungal threads of a particular mycorrhiza fungus and this is how it obtains its sustenance. The fungus, in turn, is dependent on the roots of nearby trees and shrubs, almost exclusively those of the broom honey myrtle, *Melaleuca uncinata*. In essence, both the fungus and the orchid are dependent on the shrub for survival, though the relationship between the fungus and the shrub is mutually beneficial.

Nowhere near as stupendous as the underground orchids, yet still incredible, are certain species of figs found in peninsular Malaysia, plus a few other plants around the world that flower and fruit completely underground. Slender string-like branches develop at the base of the stem or trunk and grow into the soil, where they come to resemble roots. A few flowers and figs are produced at the soil surface, while most are developed underground. Besides bearing fruit, these runner-like roots (really branches) 259

spread beneath the soil surface, where new shoots can grow from them. This can result in small thickets of the fig. Why the trees flower and fruit in this manner, and how pollination takes place underground, remains a mystery, and has to be one of the strangest known reproduction methods.

A PLANT BROUGHT BACK *to* LIFE

Bitterroot, *Lewisia rediviva*, puts on a showy, if puzzling display: each of these plants appears to consist of only a single beautiful multi-petaled flower ranging in color from pure white to soft pink. But where is the rest of the plant? Closer investigation reveals that the succulent foliage and stem are almost entirely hidden by the flower. When a large cloud passes overhead, hiding the sun, the flowers of the bitterroot fold up like umbrellas. After about a half hour, the hot sun reappears and within minutes the flowers reopen.

Rediviva means *restored to life*, an appropriate name, as we shall see. In the early 1800s, Captain Meriwether Lewis, of the Lewis and Clark North American expedition, collected a few specimens of the bitterroot in Montana. He pressed his specimens between dry papers in a botanical press and sent them to a herbarium. Many months later, in Philadelphia, a botanist was studying these now-desiccated specimens and couldn't help but notice that one of these plant's roots was showing signs of life. This specimen was

then planted and, incredibly, it started to grow. It even produced flowers the following summer!

Another source tells of a *Lewisia rediviva* plant's roots surviving after being placed in boiling water. Remarkable, if indeed true! One further note of interest about *Lewisia rediviva* is that its narrow leaves usually die after flowering, leaving thin dark threadlike remains. Yet these same

Lewisia rediviva, bitterroot VERNON SMITH

Lewisia rediviva habitat IAN GARDINER

shriveled leaves recover fully when the plant again produces flowers. The bitterroot is definitely a plant restored to life.

TOTALLY SUBMERGED *in* **SAND**

Aspens, *Populus tremula*, normally grow into fairly tall trees above ground. However, there is an amazing report of some trees on the west coast of Holland that are submerged under deep sand dunes, and yet remarkably are able to survive. All that can be seen of the trees are the uppermost twigs with emerging leaves at the tips; the rest of each tree is below a mountain of sand. Yet in a seemingly determined bid to survive against all odds, these trees continue growing.

VOLCANOES *and* PLANTS

On the volcanic Japanese island of Kyushu, some small plants of *Rhododendron kiusianum* are able to thrive among the steam and sulfur fumes. With their typical *Rhododendron*-type clusters of lilac or mauve flowers, the plants provide a display of beauty and color that is startling in such an inhospitable habitat,

Flying over to the Hawaiian Islands in the Pacific Ocean, the Ohia Lehua tree, *Metrosideros polymorpha*, can be nearly buried under the red-hot cinders of volcanic activity, but these plants are still able to sprout. Even more amazing is that new roots rapidly form just below the fresh ash surface of the volcano.

The rare Haleakala Silversword, *Argyroxiphium sandwicense* ssp. *macrocephalum*, is also native to the Hawaiian Islands. Their extremely shallow roots allow them to take hold on the dry surface of the ground that consists mostly of volcanic cinder and rock. Even though the Hawaiian Islands are most often associated with sunshine and warmth, at high altitudes the temperature can dip to freezing. How can these plants grow in such a seemingly inhospitable environment?

These hardy plants have numerous sword-like succulent leaves that are covered with shimmering silvery-blue hairs arranged in an attractive spherical formation. The plants

263

Argyroxiphium sandwicense ssp. *macrocephalum*, Haleakala silversword NEAL KRAMER

remain in this form for most of their 50-year-plus lifespan. The strong form of the plants, plus their tendency to hug the ground, allows these silverswords to resist not only the ravages of wind and cold, but also the dangers of dehydration and the sun as well. The leaves are arranged so that they and the silvery-blue hairs can raise their shoot tips by up to $36°F$ above the temperature of the surrounding

264

Argyroxiphium sandwicense ssp. *macrocephalum*, Haleakala silversword in bloom JOHN GAME

leaves. This is accomplished by focusing sunlight to converge at this point and subsequently warm the whole plant.

In a given year, zero plants may bloom, or a few thousand might. When the plants do flower, it is a special event, for this species is monocarpic, meaning the plants die after flowering. These silverswords remain compact and rounded for most of their long lives before a flower stalk even forms. But once the

265

flower stalk does develop, it reaches full maturity in just a few short weeks. After flowering, the plant's leaves become limp and dry out, the plant goes to seed and then dies. The flower stalk may stand over 6 feet tall and consists of as many as 600 maroon-colored daisy-like flower heads. Flowering usually takes place between June and July, though it sometimes extends into September.

Cephalanthera austinae, phantom orchid NEAL KRAMER

THE PHANTOM ORCHID

The phantom orchid, *Cephalanthera austinae*, flowers at widely spaced intervals. This plant is native to moist, dense forests in western North America. Its name is apt, as every part of the plant is white and the palest cream. The phantom orchid is an extremely rare species; finding one is a special event, and finding one in flower is even rarer. They bloom infrequently, sometimes only once every 16 years.

AFTERWORD

All of the weird and wonderful adaptations we've seen demonstrate plants' amazing drive to survive and spread their progeny. Some of the most successful are labeled as weeds: the familiar dandelion is one such plant, but there are many more. Invasive plants are most often alien species that have become abundant and widespread to the point of aggressively suffocating native species. This can negatively affect natural ecosystems including not only plant life, but animal life as well, and it can have economic implications for us, too.

Thankfully there are concerned invasive-plant societies in many regions. These organizations identify invasive plant species and ways and means to bring them under control or even eradicate them. Complementary organizations include native plant societies that focus on identifying and conserving native plant species.

For those who want to know more about the environmental, ecological and conservation concerns surrounding plant life around the world, several other organizations are recommended for further research.

- The International Union for the Conservation of Nature (IUCN) maintains "red lists" that include threat categories for plants — threatened, endangered, critically endangered, vulnerable and extinct.
- The Convention on International Trade in Endangered Species of Wild Fauna and Flora (CITES) monitors and controls international trade in threatened animals and plants.
- The United Nations Educational, Scientific and Cultural Organization (UNESCO) includes World Natural Heritage Sites, such as the Socotra archipelago, where one finds many plants existing nowhere else on earth.
- The World Wildlife Fund (WWF) has a Global 200 list that identifies regions crucial to the conservation of global biodiversity — worldwide hotspots and ecoregions with rich and unique biological diversity.
- Conservation International also has a list of

268

biodiversity hotspots — ecological areas that are unusually rich in their fauna and flora species, often unique to that area.

- The Global Strategy for Plant Conservation (GSPC) is the first global agreement with clear conservation strategies developed by the Convention on Biological Diversity (CBD).
- CBD promotes conservation and the sustainable use of plants and animals.

Other organizations worth investigating further include botanical gardens as well as international, national and regional botanical conservation bodies.

Through such research, you will learn more about the remarkable world of plants, as well as the crucial related ecological and environmental issues.

SELECTED SOURCES

Attenborough, David, *The Private Life of Plants* (Princeton, NJ: Princeton University Press, 1995).

Australian Government Department of the Environment, Flora Databases and Online Resources, www.environment.gov.au/biodiversity/abrs/online-resources/flora/index.html (accessed June 23, 2014).

Bailey, L. H., and Ethel Zoe Bailey, *Hortus Third: A Concise Dictionary of Plants Cultivated in the United States and Canada* (New York, NY: Macmillan Publishing Co. Inc., 1978).

Baker, Dr. Robin, ed., *The Mystery of Migration* (Toronto, ON: John Wiley & Sons Canada, 1980).

Bell, Peter R., and C. L. Woodcock, *The Diversity of Green Plants* (Reading, MA: Addison-Wesley, 1968).

Burnie, David, *Tree* (New York, NY: Alfred A. Knopf Publishers, 1988).

The California Department of Forestry and Fire Protection, www.fire.ca.gov (accessed June 23, 2014).

Canadian Museum of Nature, nature.ca/en/home (accessed June 23, 2014).

Carder, Al, *Forest Giants of the World: Past and Present* (Markham, ON: Fitzhenry & Whiteside, 1995).

Clark, Lewis J., *Wild Flowers of the Pacific Northwest* (Sidney, BC: Gray's Publishing Ltd., 1976).

Cooke, M. C., *Freaks and Marvels of Plant Life, or Curiosities of Vegetation* (New York, NY: E. & J.B. Young & Co., 1882).

271

Corner, E. J. H., *The Life of Plants* (New York, NY: New American Library, 1968).

Daubenmire, R. F., *Plants and Environment* (Toronto, ON: John Wiley & Sons, 1974).

Douglas, G. W., and J. Pojar, eds., *Illustrated Flora of British Columbia, Vol. 6,* Monocotyledons Acoraceae *through* Najadaceae (Victoria, BC: Ministry of Environment, Lands and Parks/BC Ministry of Forests, 2001).

E-Flora BC: Electronic Atlas of the Flora of British Columbia, www.geog.ubc.ca/biodiversity/eflora/index .shtml (accessed June 23, 2014).

Everett, Thomas H., *Living Trees of the World* (New York, NY: Chanticleer Press, 1968).

Frankton, Clarence, and Gerald A. Mulligan, *Weeds of Canada* (Ottawa, ON: Canada Dept. of Agriculture, 1980).

Gildemeister, Heidi, *Mediterranean Gardening: A Waterwise Approach* (Oakland, CA: University of California Press, 2002).

Goss, James A., *Physiology of Plants and Their Cells* (Oxford, UK: Pergamon Press, 1973).

Greulach, V. A., and J. Edison Adams, *Plants: An Introduction to Modern Botany* (New York, NY: John Wiley & Sons, 1976).

Hart, James W., *Plant Tropisms and Other Growth Movements* (London, UK: Chapman & Hall, 1990).

Hewes, Jeremy Joan, *Redwoods: The World's Largest Trees* (Chicago, IL: Rand McNally & Co., 1981).

Heywood, V. H., and S. R. Chant, eds., *Popular Encyclopedia of Plants* (Cambridge, UK: Cambridge University Press, 1982).

Hickey, M., and C. J. King, *100 Families of Flowering Plants* (Cambridge, UK: Cambridge University Press, 1981).

Himmelman, Duncan, *Botanica* (Richmond, BC: Raincoast Books, 1998).

Hora, Bayard, *The Oxford Encyclopaedia of Trees of the World* (Oxford, UK: Oxford University Press, 1981).

273

Hosie, R. C., *Native Trees of Canada* (Ottawa, ON: Canadian Forestry Service, 1969).

Huxley, Anthony Julian, *Green Inheritance* (London, UK: William Collins and Sons, 1984).

———, *Plant and Planet* (New York, NY: The Viking Press Inc., 1974).

The International Plant Names Index, www.ipni.org/index.html (accessed June 23, 2014).

Johnson, Hugh, *Hugh Johnson's Encyclopedia of Trees* (New York, NY: Gallery Books, 1984).

Jones, David A., and Dennis A. Wilkens, *Variations and Adaptations in Plant Species* (New York: Crane-Russak, 1971).

Kerner von Marilaun, Anton; F. W. Oliver, trans. & ed., *The Natural History of Plants: Their Forms, Growth, Reproduction and Distribution* (London, UK: Blackie & Son Ltd., 1894).

Kew Royal Botanic Gardens, Millennium Seed Bank Project, www.kew.org/science-conservation/millennium

-seed-bank-partnership / about-millennium-seed-bank -partnership (accessed June 23, 2014).

Little, Elbert L., *The Audubon Society Field Guide to North American Trees: Western Region* (New York, NY: Alfred A. Knopf Inc., 1980).

Marinelli, Janet, ed., *Plant* (Toronto, ON: Dorling Kindersley, 2005).

Menninger, Edwin A., *Fantastic Trees* (Portland, OR: Timber Press, 1995).

Merrill, E. D., *Plant Life of the Pacific World* (New York, NY: Macmillan, 1946).

Mitchell Beazley International, eds., *The International Book of the Forest* (New York, NY: Simon & Shuster, 1981).

Muller, Fritz, *The Living Arctic* (Toronto, ON: Methuen, 1981).

Nicholson, Barbara E., and Arthur R. Clapman, *The Oxford Book of Trees* (Oxford, UK: Oxford University Press, 1975).

275

Noble, Park S., *Remarkable Agaves and Cacti* (New York, NY: Oxford University Press, 1994).

Palgrave, Keith Coates, *Trees of Southern Africa* (Capetown, South Africa: Struik Publishers, 1986).

Perry, Frances, *Flowers of the World* (London, UK: Hamlyn Publishing Group, Ltd., 1972).

Prance, Ghillean Tolmie, *Leaves* (New York, NY: Crown, 1985).

Prasad, M. N. V., ed., *Plant Ecophysiology* (New York, NY: John Wiley & Sons, 1996).

Schnell, Donald E., *Carnivorous Plants of the United States and Canada* (Portland, OR: Timber Press, 2002).

Schulman, Edmund, "Bristlecone Pine, Oldest Living Thing" (*National Geographic*, March 1958, 355-372).

Suzuki, David, and Wayne Grady, *Tree: A Life Story* (Vancouver, BC: Greystone Books, 2004).

Szczawinski, F. W., *The Orchids of British Columbia* (Victoria, BC: British Columbia Provincial Museum Handbook No. 16, 1975).

Tree Atlas of Namibia, treeatlas.biodiversity.org.na/fullist .php (accessed June 23, 2014).

Turk, Jonathan, and Amos Turk, *Environmental Science* (Philadelphia, PA: Saunders College Publishing, 1978).

Went, F. W., *The Plants* (Morristown, NJ: Silver Bundett, 1963).

Wharton, David, *Life at the Limits: Organisms in Extreme Environments* (Cambridge, UK: Cambridge University Press, 2002).

Wildscreen Arkive, www.arkive.org/plants-and-algae (accessed June 23, 2014).

Willis, J. C., *A Dictionary of the Flowering Plants and Ferns* (Cambridge, UK: Cambridge University Press, 1966).

277

RECOMMENDED BOOKS AND WEBSITES

Alaska Wildflowers, www.alaskawildflowers.us (accessed June 23, 2014) — incredible photographs of several plants discussed in this book.

Clark, Lewis J., *Wild Flowers of the Pacific Northwest* (Sidney, BC: Gray's Publishing Ltd., 1976) — a great resource with an almost poetic presentation.

Conservation International Hotspots, www.conservation .org/How/Pages/Hotspots.aspx.

The Convention on Biological Diversity (CBD), www.cbd.int.

Convention on International Trade in Endangered Species of Wild Fauna and Flora (CITES), www.cites.org.

E-Flora BC: Electronic Atlas of the Flora of British Columbia, www.geog.ubc.ca/biodiversity/eflora/index .shtml (accessed June 23, 2014) — excellent information and photographs focusing on native and naturalized plants in British Columbia and vicinity.

International Union for the Conservation of Nature (IUCN), www.iucn.org.

Marinelli, Janet, ed., *Plant* (Toronto, ON: Dorling Kindersley, 2005) — a distinctive book that focuses on conserving plants and their environments around the world.

Menninger, Edwin A., *Fantastic Trees* (Portland, OR: Timber Press, 1995) — a wonderful book focusing mainly on tropical trees.

National Park Service (Hawaii), www.nps.gov/hale/ naturescience/silversword.htm (accessed June 23, 2014) — great photographs and further information on silverswords.

San Francisco Botanical Garden, www.sfbotanicalgarden
.org/garden/bloom_11_09.shtml (accessed June 23, 2014)
— great photographs and further information on *Passiflora
parritae*.

The United Nations Educational, Scientific and Cultural
Organization (UNESCO), whc.unesco.org/en/list —
includes World Natural Heritage Sites.

Wayne's Word, www.waynes-word.com — a plentiful
source of plant information.

Wildscreen Arkive, www.arkive.org/plants-and-algae
(accessed June 23, 2014) — excellent photographs and
extensive information.

The World Wildlife Fund (WWF) Global 200 List,
www.panda.org.

ADDITIONAL PHOTO CREDITS

Page 6: Icy *Saussurea gossypiphora*, shot in the Himalaya; Prateek (greatestprateek@gmail.com); Creative Commons Attribution-Share Alike 2.5 Generic license; creativecommons.org/licenses/by-sa/2.5/legalcode; commons.wikimedia.org/wiki/File:Saussurea_gossypiphora_Himalaya.jpg

Page 30: Hura crepitans, sandbox tree at Puentes Colgantes near Arenal Volcano, Costa Rica; Hans Hillewaert; Creative Commons Attribution-Share Alike 4.0 International; creativecommons.org/licenses/by-sa/4.0/; commons.wikimedia.org/wiki/File:Hura_crepitans_%28fruit%29.jpg

281

Page 58: Pachypodium rosulatum gracilius in the Isalo National Park, Madagascar; Bernard Gagnon; Creative Commons Attribution-Share Alike 3.0 Unported, 2.5 Generic, 2.0 Generic and 1.0 Generic license; GNU Free Documentation License; creativecommons.org/licenses/by-sa/3.0/legalcode; creativecommons.org/licenses/by-sa/2.0/legalcode; creativecommons.org/licenses/by-sa/1.0/legalcode; commons.wikimedia.org/wiki/Commons:GNU_Free_Documentation_License,_version_1.2; commons.wikimedia.org/wiki/File:Pachypodium_Rosulatum_Gracilius_01.jpg

Page 62: Adansonia grandidieri, Madagascar baobab; Bernard Gagnon; Creative Commons Attribution-Share Alike 3.0 Unported, 2.5 Generic, 2.0 Generic and 1.0 Generic license; GNU Free Documentation License; commons.wikimedia.org/wiki/File:Adansonia_grandidieri04.jpg

Page 151: Ficus benghalensis, Indian banyan tree; Delonix; Creative Commons Attribution-Share Alike 3.0 Unported; commons.wikimedia.org/wiki/File:Banyan_Tree_at_The_Valley_School_,_Bangalore.JPG

Page 154: Ficus aurea, strangler fig butresses at Rincon de la Vieja, Costa Rica; Hans Hillewaert; Creative Commons Attribution-Share Alike 3.0 Unported; commons.wikimedia.org/wiki/File:Ficus_aurea_%28butresses%29.jpg

INDEX OF PLANTS

284

QUIVER
TREES

286

287

288

ACKNOWLEDGMENTS

Most importantly, I would like to thank Jack David, publisher of ECW Press, for believing in this special project. I would also like to thank all the awesome people at ECW Press as well as everyone else who was involved in producing this book in such an artistic and professional manner. You are an incredible team! Individual personal thanks go to: Erin Creasey, Jen Knoch, Laura Pastore, Rachel Ironstone, Troy Cunningham, Lynn Gammie, Samantha Dobson, Crissy Calhoun and Stuart Ross.

I would also like to thank all of the many photographers who contributed their excellent high-quality photo images for the book. Their stunning photos truly augment the text well.